'This is a comprehensive and extremely useful book about the toileting difficulties associated with Autism Spectrum Disorders. From developing basic toilet training and independence skills to discussing more complex issues like sensory differences, constipation, smearing and avoidant behaviour the book clearly demonstrates the importance of understanding how autism impacts on these difficulties. It offers practical, tried and tested suggestions and includes useful resources and links. This is going to be an invaluable book that has successfully drawn together, for the first time, everything you need to know about this subject.'

– Suzie Franklin, Author, Personalisation in Practice, *and Family Liaison, Inscape House School*

'I was delighted to be asked to review this excellent book which gives a common sense and practical approach to toilet training children with ASD. By debunking the myth that toilet training should be delayed until the child "is ready" it ensures that all children with ASD are given the same opportunities as their peers. I would suggest that this book should be essential reading for all those involved with the care of such children.'

– June Rogers MBE, PromoCon Paediatric Continence Specialist

'This is a 'must-have' book. A comprehensive, informative and easy-to-read guide through the difficulties of toilet training individuals with ASD, this book is helpful for professionals and parents alike. It is thorough and full of practical, tried and tested ideas. The use of parent views makes this an excellent resource.'

– Lizi Snushall, Senior Teacher at Uffculme School (ASD specific), Birmingham

of related interest

Liam Goes Poo in the Toilet
A Story about Trouble with Toilet Training
Jane Whelen Banks
ISBN 978 1 84310 900 6
eISBN 978 1 84642 874 6

Fun with Messy Play
Ideas and Activities for Children with Special Needs
Tracy Beckerleg
ISBN 978 1 84310 641 8
eISBN 978 1 84642 854 8

Make Your Own Picture Stories for Kids with ASD (Autism Spectrum Disorder)
A DIY Guide for Parents and Carers
Brian Attwood
ISBN 978 1 84905 638 0
eISBN 978 1 78450 117 4

Helping Children with Autism Spectrum Conditions through Everyday Transitions
Small Changes - Big Challenges
John Smith, Jane Donlan and Bob Smith
ISBN 978 1 84905 275 7
eISBN 978 0 85700 572 4

Toilet Training
and the Autism Spectrum (ASD)

A Guide for Professionals

Dr Eve Fleming MB ChB BA MRCPCH
and Lorraine MacAlister PGC Autism, BSc Psychology

Foreword by Dr Penny Dobson MBE

Jessica Kingsley *Publishers*
London and Philadelphia

Bristol Stool Chart on p.112 is reproduced with kind permission from Dr KW Heaton, formerly Reader in Medicine at the University of Bristol. © 2000 produced by Norgine Pharmaceuticals Limited.

First published in 2016
by Jessica Kingsley Publishers
73 Collier Street
London N1 9BE, UK
and
400 Market Street, Suite 400
Philadelphia, PA 19106, USA

www.jkp.com

Library of Congress Cataloging in Publication Data
A CIP catalog record for this book is available from the Library of Congress

British Library Cataloguing in Publication Data
A CIP catalogue record for this book is available from the British Library

ISBN 978 1 84905 603 8
eISBN 978 1 78450 070 2

Printed and bound in Great Britain

MIX
Paper from
responsible sources
FSC® C013056

We would like to dedicate this book to all the children with autism and their parents from whom we have learned so much about learning to use the toilet. We have enjoyed their challenges and individuality.

CONTENTS

PART 3 WEE AND POO: MANUFACTURE, STORAGE AND TRANSIT

PART 4 UNDERSTANDING BEHAVIOUR

FOREWORD

Children with autism spectrum disorders often find toilet training a challenge – as do their parents and carers. Yet, for the vast majority, continence *can* be achieved. Health and allied professionals – including health visitors, school and nursery nurses, as well as members of the more specialist paediatric continence team – play an important role in advising and supporting parents in their journey towards their child becoming fully toilet trained. The good news is that this new publication equips the professional to take on this task with confidence. Not only does it provide up-to-date information, but it has plenty of practical suggestions to engage the families concerned.

My pleasure at being asked to write this foreword is personal as well as professional, as my parents were among a small group of founder members of the National Autistic Society – and my father, Geoffrey Dobson OBE, was the Society's second chairman. I, on the other hand, was the founder director of the national charity ERIC (Education and Resources for Improving Childhood Continence), which I set up 1987 until handing it over as an established organisation to a new director twenty-one years later.

I feel confident that this much-needed publication will be disseminated widely and will prove an essential tool for professionals nationally.

Dr Penny Dobson MBE

ACKNOWLEDGEMENTS

We would like to acknowledge the help of Dr Jacqueline Knibbs, Consultant Clinical Psychologist, for all her advice and guidance, particularly for her help with the section on compliance difficulties and PDA.

Our thanks go to Jacqui and Jack Eames for sharing their experiences with us and allowing us to share these with readers.

We would like to thank the following people for their support and help with reviewing the book: Ruth Hunt, Pauline Partridge, Carol Baker, Dr Penny Dobson, Suzie Franklin, Patrick Fleming, Mandy Rutter and Steven Owens.

Our thanks also go to Lola Fleming for her ideas and image for the cover design.

We would also like to extend our thanks for all the stories and ideas given to us on the courses we have delivered for The National Autistic Society on learning to wee and poo in the right place.

PART 1

UNDERSTANDING TOILET TRAINING AND AUTISM

Chapter 1

INTRODUCTION

What this book is about

Parents and families often struggle with toilet training, especially when children have difficulties such as autism. In this book we provide professionals with ideas and resources to enable them to give information and support for children, parents and carers.

Toilet training is not just about coming out of nappies, pads and continence protection. It includes the wide range of skills a child needs to become reliably clean and dry and acquire reliable control of their bowel and bladder. There are a range of difficulties that may arise during the teaching of reliable continence skills; these may be ongoing or develop at a later stage. We aim to provide a structure for professionals to evaluate and understand these difficulties and provide effective solutions.

Preparation

This is perhaps the most important factor in ensuring that toilet training is successful. We explore how to make effective preparation, evaluate readiness and plan when and how to begin toilet training programmes.

Practicalities

Throughout this book we emphasise the importance of a holistic approach to assessment and intervention for difficulties with toilet training. Children will often have different starting points and problems, so plans to help develop skills to use the toilet need to be individualised. Targets often need to be prioritised and learning simplified into a stepwise approach.

Problem solving

Difficulties often arise through the toilet training journey and we discuss the need to evaluate the factors contributing to these in order to help in creating appropriate solutions. Often problems with toilet training reflect underlying difficulties, including stress and anxiety, which may need to be the initial focus for intervention.

Progress

This is unique for each individual and needs to focus on the child or young person becoming as independent as possible. At times a child may make rapid progress, and once they have learned to use the toilet then they continue with confidence and reliability. Often progress may be more gradual, and both families and professionals need to be patient, creative and consistent.

With the right input, children with autism can nearly always be toilet trained. Success is possible and should be celebrated!

Our perspectives

Eve: a community children's doctor

Recently I received an email from a parent who I first met some time ago when her son was five and he had difficulties with toilet training. At the time relationships with staff in his primary school had been very tense and frustrated, so his parents decided they had to change his school. Jack, now aged 15 included his views in the email and said:

> 'The hardest part of dealing with it was that it prevented me from doing activities, such as swimming, at my first school,

which from my point of view was just random rules enforced by adults. It never embarrassed me in any way. I just saw it as how it was.'

It occurred to me that no one had explained to Jack at the time why he couldn't go swimming, and why there was this rule. He would have been quite capable of understanding this. We tried hard to encourage his toileting with routines, reminders and rewards, but I do not think we were successful in understanding how Jack saw things. This can often be difficult, but adults seem rarely to try to find out what children think; they are often too busy trying to tell them what they want them to do. This emphasises the focus of this book: that to help children and families we need to think about every aspect of the toilet training process and learn to be creative. It is important to consider children's perspectives as well as the view of their families, carers and other professionals.

In the mid-1960s, as a recently qualified doctor, I began working in a general practice in Brixton as a trainee. The partners were inspirational and taught me so much about health problems and their complexity, as well as about general practice. One of the partners, Margaret Pollack, was very interested in child development. I found this area fascinating, especially as my first child was then under one year old. In those days, child development had only been mentioned briefly at medical school, and the understanding of it in medicine was a new field.

I later set up developmental clinics for children in other practices where I worked. I had learned from Margaret Pollack that children and families could be helped most when delays were identified early.

As my family grew older I moved from general practice to work in community child health and this included seeing many children who had developmental delay and special needs. I worked closely with many other agencies and therapists, including education, psychology, speech and language therapy, and social services. I learned a great deal from these professionals and recognised the importance of working together to help children and families.

As part of my role in the community I was asked to run clinics to help children with continence difficulties, and also to give advice and supervision to the school nurses who supported children in their schools with wetting and soiling difficulties. I found that helping children and families with these problems made a significant difference to children's lives and provided great relief for their families. As well as improvement in continence, there was often a profound impact on children's emotional wellbeing as well as their confidence and learning in school. I remember a boy of ten, who had been receiving treatment for some time for behavioural difficulties; I assessed and treated his constipation and bowel incontinence successfully. He came to see me for review and said, 'You have changed my life.' This brought home to me how great an impact these difficulties have on children, although this may not always be apparent at first.

I often found it appeared that the children were unaware of and uninterested in wetting and soiling. It was only when this improved that it became obvious that their apparent lack of interest was in fact a reflection of their feelings of disappointment and frustration caused by their wetting and soiling difficulties. Frequently, parents and teachers were surprised and impressed by the improvement in children's behaviour and education when continence difficulties were addressed.

Quite a few of the children attending the clinic had problems with delayed development and autistic patterns of behaviour. I worked closely with my psychology colleagues and we set up joint clinics to develop coordinated strategies to help these children. I also learned a great deal about autism and how to support children and families. We spent time with parents and education staff to make sure that everyone understood the child's needs and developed joint approaches and consistency. Often, some of our suggestions needed to be scheduled and adapted to accommodate other social and educational needs. We quickly learned that children did significantly better in schools where there was understanding and commitment to joint working. We were often impressed with how dedicated and resourceful many school staff were; and discussing a child's needs helped everyone to gain a better insight into their difficulties.

My experiences have led me to become aware of the value of a joint approach to assessment and intervention, with parents and carers the key people in the team. The understanding of the physical aspects of continence difficulties alongside the behavioural factors is essential to developing a holistic approach that is necessary for a successful outcome. I also learned that you have to think creatively to develop effective programmes for children on the autism spectrum, and individual approaches were needed.

One breakthrough success was for a little boy when his mother found some dinosaur stickers at the Natural History Museum, as like many children with autism he had a special interest, which for him was fossils and dinosaurs. His response was magical!

Sometimes there were children who were coming to the clinic for a long time, and our progress was slow. One little boy had been coming from the time he was five. Over the years, he been diagnosed with autism and ADHD, received a statement of special educational needs, as well as bowel training programmes, reminders and rewards, and constipation treatment. It was a great day for all of us when he came to the clinic aged ten, with a bunch of flowers and a huge grin, and said, 'I don't need you any more!' His expression said everything about the importance of this to him and why this work was so rewarding for me.

Lorraine – an autism training consultant

My interest in autism started early and has always been with me. My mum was a children's nurse who ran summer play-schemes for children with disabilities for many years and that was where I spent my summer holidays from a very early age! A few of the children attending the play-schemes had been diagnosed with autism, and they clearly had a way of seeing the world that was very different from others. I found myself naturally gravitating towards these particular children as I found their behaviours and outlook fascinating.

This early experience made me want to work with people with autism. I gained a degree in psychology, and then worked in residential services for adults with autism, and after that at a local autism organisation supporting children and families.

I joined The National Autistic Society (NAS) in 2005, and delivered the *Help!* programme. This was a post-diagnostic family support programme, which included a range of topics such as understanding autism, sensory needs, managing anger, understanding behaviour, and teen and adult life. One of the seminars we started in 2007 was on Common Toileting Difficulties. This was a topic I found absolutely fascinating!

I quickly realised that toileting and its linked difficulties are rarely talked about openly but caused enormous difficulties for families. We developed a seminar to support families who had children with continence difficulties, working with Janet Blannin from ERIC and then June Rogers from PromoCon to develop this programme. The key principle with both organisations was to bring our autism knowledge alongside their continence knowledge, in order to support children and their families. Discussions with Janet and June confirmed my belief that children with autism can almost always be successfully toilet trained, but for some individuals it may take more time and preparation.

Looking back on my time working in residential services supporting adults with autism, I remember we were often advised to take people to the toilet every 30 minutes, which did not seem to work at all, and this is still done in some settings for both children and adults. At that time I was not aware of the range of treatments for constipation and the need for individualised toileting programmes. I have seen at first hand that, in the short term, often the easier option is to keep a person in nappies.

As an autism practitioner and trainer, I have continued to develop my knowledge about toilet training and how to help families. One of the most important things I have learnt has been an understanding of the bowel and bladder, and the need to consider this alongside the impact of the autism on learning toilet training skills. This knowledge has dispelled the myth that children or adults with autism and severe learning disabilities cannot be toilet trained.

From a non-medical perspective, I have had to learn more about the difficulties of identifying constipation in children. This is one of the most common issues that arise on both the parental and professional courses I have been involved in delivering, and we are still hearing about individuals where it has not been identified and addressed properly.

I've now realised that engaging in an open discussion about toileting issues can initiate the ability for both parents and professionals to share concerns about a range of intimate and care issues that have not been talked about before. The opportunity to discuss frankly and openly the difficulties individuals may be having enables them to receive the help and support they need.

A parent's perspective

I found that having a child with autism demanded contact with many agencies, and at times created conflicting situations with schools. Sometimes the huge amount of communicating, mediating and diplomatic interventions needed seemed entirely overwhelming and totally exhausting. When this includes toileting issues in addition, it can feel like the last straw. Even an invitation to tea from another family can be enormously stressful: do you mention the toileting issues (embarrassing and difficult) or just keep your fingers crossed that all goes well? Jack had difficulties several times a day, most days, and for very many years, so the 'hoping for the best' route didn't seem an option, and we had many tricky conversations with people who didn't understand, including education professionals who should have known better. I remember a particularly upsetting conversation with a school governor when our child was in the reception class; she phoned me one evening to ask me why I hadn't toilet trained my son before he started school. My response was to want to keep Jack close and hide from the world, which wouldn't have been a helpful thing in terms of developing his social skills, or in terms of my sanity. So we just had to plough on regardless.

What helped was the support we received from the local bowel and bladder clinic where we were given encouragement and reassurance. It was only in the context of these meetings that the problem seemed normal. One of the most useful things was to be reminded that Jack would grow out of this phase, and that by the time he was in his teens, even if it was still an issue, it would be one he would deal with himself! And of course, the problem did eventually resolve. Now, as my son enters his GCSE year, those issues seem like a dim and distant memory.

Although we were helped to develop strategies to encourage Jack to stay clean and dry, in fact I found that very little we did made much difference. The only thing we could do was to keep fuss (either positive or negative) to a minimum, as this just seemed to make things worse. What worked best was to equip ourselves to cope (we still find spare pants and nappy sacks in coats we haven't worn in years). In a weird way, it helped me just to accept it as part of our lives and not strive too much to change it, as I found it hard to cope with the disappointment of a relapse and it made me frustrated with Jack. So for us, acceptance and tolerance combined with being prepared got us through.

Chapter 2

THE IMPORTANCE OF TOILET TRAINING

Learning to use the toilet is one of the most important skills a child can learn and has a large impact on the child, their family and friends, and the professionals involved. Each child should be supported to reach their full potential in terms of the skills they are able to develop, and this will have significant benefit on their self-esteem, relationships and future opportunities.

Worldwide toileting

Wee and poo occurs in all people, and in all cultures children are trained to become continent. There is, though, a variation in facilities, resources, customs and attitudes. The different cultural perspectives, attitudes and practices need to be understood and considered in planning and creating programmes to help children with autism to learn toileting skills.

What is toilet training?

Toilet training involves learning to understand the actions, language and routines involved in learning to use the toilet, and developing skills and independence in managing these.

This can be a challenge for many children with autism. A combination of difficulties or limitations in physical development, bowel and bladder functioning, communication, understanding, and sensory differences can all play their part in making learning new skills difficult. It often causes significant stress for the child, parents and carers.

Children with autism may experience a range of difficulties related to toileting. There may be physical problems with the maturity or functioning of the bladder or bowel, which are unrelated to their autism. Other difficulties may be specifically linked to their autism and delays in development and understanding. There will often be components from more than one area, and attention to all the contributing factors is essential to developing appropriate strategies to achieve success. These will all be explored in more detail throughout the book.

Why is it so important?

Parents often identify toileting difficulties as a priority, and this is an area they often find extremely challenging. The significant advantages for children of being toilet trained include an increase in confidence, independence and self-esteem, and opportunities for recreational and fun activities, education and social interaction. There can be a reduction in isolation and in the risk of being bullied. For parents there are also rewards in the satisfaction of helping their child achieve this skill. There is also a reduction in the stress of continued changing and cleaning and having to plan for access to changing facilities, which is often particularly difficult with older children. Life can become relatively more relaxed. There will also be a significant reduction in the time and costs involved with nappies, bedding and constant washing. The time saved can then be available for other activities. For education and care staff, life with a child that is clean and dry is much easier, as well as creating more time to teach other skills and learning objectives.

The idea of toilet training can be very daunting. Parents may assume this means the nappy will be taken away immediately. This book tries to emphasise and address the support needs of parents and the need to plan carefully and break down the task into easy, manageable stages.

It is often found that leaving a child in a nappy is an easier management strategy than implementing a toileting programme. This is not helpful and does not address a young person's needs, or promote their dignity and autonomy.

'It is much easier just to change the pads rather than stick with the toileting routine.' (*Senior Support Worker, residential service for young people with autism*)

Many parents will begin the process of toilet training around the age of two years. Some children may have received a diagnosis of autism by this time, but many children will not yet have had a full assessment and diagnosis. The age of diagnosis of autism in the UK varies considerably, with the earliest being given at eighteen months old but more frequently not until school age or older. The average age of diagnosis in the UK is 5½ years; this rises to 11 years in those with Asperger syndrome (Howlin and Asgharian 1999). Even before a diagnosis, most families or caregivers will have recognised that the child is having difficulties, although they may be unsure of the underlying cause. Some families have tried toilet training which has been unsuccessful, and have found it a distressing and stressful experience for all. They then abandon it, thinking they will return to it at a later date. Many families have said that when their child did receive a diagnosis of autism, this helped to explain why the child reacted so negatively to the first attempts at toilet training.

Some families who have a child with a diagnosis of autism or learning disability may be advised by professionals to postpone toilet training until their child is 'more settled'. This advice is usually to relieve the stress on parents, but it may postpone training unnecessarily. It is often more helpful to offer support and discuss initial steps. Parents need accurate advice, information and ongoing support. It is essential to remember that the longer a child has to establish behaviour, the more difficult it can be to change this in the future. The evaluation of toilet-readiness will be discussed later in the book.

'My child had spent ten years doing everything in his nappy, so getting him to start changing that was very difficult.' (*Parent of a child with autism*)

Children, parents and carers will all need ongoing advice and support through the learning process. This is needed from the early stages of preparation and assessment of readiness, through the development and implementation of a toileting programme and trouble-shooting any problems along the way, towards celebrating success.

Chapter 3

WHY TOILET TRAINING IS DIFFICULT FOR CHILDREN ON THE AUTISM SPECTRUM

There is no right time or right way of toilet training.

It is important to say that although difficulties with toileting are common in children with autism, quite a number of them learn to use the toilet successfully at around the usual time. In addition, many children who do not have autism often have some difficulty in developing reliable continence skills. It is important to point out that the age of learning bowel and bladder control varies a great deal.

Nevertheless, many children with autism find it difficult to learn toileting skills, and they sometimes acquire these later than other children. This is because behaviours linked to their autism, developmental skills, family issues and physical factors may create difficulties in learning continence. These factors may be relevant individually, but also frequently interact. This book will focus on the need to evaluate all the components of toileting to develop the most effective strategies to help children learn this skill.

It is essential that professionals who support and give advice to children with autism and their families have an understanding of how to assess the different factors that may contribute to difficulties with toilet training. This will ensure that the medical professionals consider the autism, the professionals in the autism field think about the possibility of physical difficulties, and both arrange further evaluation if needed.

The majority of children with autism do become continent and learn to use the toilet, although it can sometimes be a difficult journey. There is no right time or right way of toilet training, and we will be discussing the need to try to develop a programme that is right for the individual needs of the child and also considers the needs of the family and others.

Family needs

The right time for a family to embark on toilet training will vary greatly depending on the family situation. The needs of parents and other family members should always be considered in deciding when to start teaching a child to use the toilet. Some children may still be going through the autism assessment and diagnosis process, and this may impact upon the whole family. They often need time to absorb and adjust to the implications of an autism diagnosis before embarking on teaching a child a new and complex skill. Parents should not feel pressurised to start toilet training; an understanding of the family dynamics is essential, including emotional, health, social, employment, financial and other issues. If there is anything that is creating stress and anxiety for a family, battling with wee and poo will almost always make things worse!

Developmental progress

Many children with autism have delay in one or more areas of development. The principal area affected is social development, but other areas may also be delayed, such as language, understanding or motor skills, and several areas of learning can be involved. It is necessary to assess a child's development in all areas to understand their difficulties in learning the complex skill of achieving continence. Help with other developmental skills may make a good foundation to build on to acquire other new skills, as well as helping parents and carers gain confidence in supporting their child. Developmental delays can make toileting skills more difficult to learn, and it is frequently important to discuss their needs with therapists and teachers who know the child.

It is fairly common that often developmental and behavioural concerns take priority. Toilet training may be easier when other developmental skills such as communication have been acquired and supported.

Autism

Autism is a lifelong developmental disability that affects the way people understand, and interact with the world around them. The National Autistic Society explains that it is a spectrum condition, which means that, while all people with autism share certain difficulties, their condition will affect them in different ways, including a variation in severity. Some people with autism are able to live relatively independent lives but others may have accompanying learning disabilities and need a lifetime of specialist support.[1]

In 1979 Lorna Wing and Judith Gould identified the three core difficulties that people with autism present: social communication, social interaction and social imagination. They introduced the term Autism Spectrum Disorder (ASD). More recently, the incidence and importance of sensory differences has become increasingly appreciated. Asperger syndrome is a form of autism where people are often of average or above average intelligence, have fewer problems with speech but may still have difficulties with understanding and processing language.

Problems with social communication

Children with autism have difficulties with social communication. This can include not understanding how to use words or what different words mean, not using and understanding facial expressions and body language, not reading faces, and not understanding and using verbal and non-verbal communication.

---

1   www.autism.org.uk

This could mean they may not understand what they are being asked to do, and they may take things literally and find it hard to communicate the need to go to the toilet.

A great deal of language used about toileting is often confusing:

'Let's spend a penny.'

'Go for a tinkle.'

'Pop yourself on the toilet.'

'Sit on the toilet.'

The different signs and pictures that are used to label toilets can be difficult to interpret for some children. Door signs that indicate either men's, women's or accessible toilets can take time to process and are all slightly different.

These problems with understanding mean that it is vitally important to use clear and consistent communication. It is necessary to decide on what words or phrases you are going to use related to toileting, and try to get everyone involved to use the same. Going to the 'toilet' at school, the 'loo' at home and the 'lavatory' at your auntie's house can be incredibly confusing!

Problems with social interaction

Children with autism have difficulties in social interaction. This can include not recognising or understanding other people's emotions and feelings or expressing their own. They may have difficulties relating and interacting with others or in understanding unwritten rules.

One of the main difficulties that children with autism have is in understanding social behaviour and cues, so unlike other children they do not have the motivation to copy others, conform to expectation or want to be grown up. This could mean they are less likely to learn new skills, may not be socially motivated to wear 'big boy' or 'big girl' pants or use the toilet as their peers do. They may be less motivated to please parents and caregivers by weeing or pooing in the right place, and may not mind if they are wet or soiled, or understand why parents and carers do mind.

There may be some children with autism who find direct praise difficult to understand or accept. This needs to be considered, as traditional approaches to toilet training usually include giving very obvious praise when a child uses the toilet correctly for the first time. This emphasises the importance of understanding the individual child and how their autism affects their responses as well as their understanding.

Problems with social imagination

Children with autism have difficulties in social imagination. This can include not being able to understand and predict other people's behaviour, make sense of what is happening around them, and imagine situations that they have not experienced or cope with change. Many children can also have intense fascinations or special interests based around certain objects or subjects, and they may regard other things as unimportant.

Simon Baron-Cohen (2008) discusses how some children with autism are delayed in developing a theory of mind. This can mean that such children find it difficult to put themselves in someone else's shoes, to imagine their thoughts and feelings in order to make sense of and predict their behaviour. For some children, because they know they need the toilet, they may think that the adults around them also know this, therefore they do not realise the need to communicate it.

Many children with autism may be confused about what the bathroom is for. Some may think it is just for bathing and washing and may not understand that it is also the place that they should go to use the toilet. Many children who are in nappies continue to have their nappy changed in a different place; this could be the bedroom or lounge at home, or the medical room at school. Many children with autism associate specific places with specific tasks, therefore we may need to begin teaching them that the toilet in the bathroom is the place where we do our wee and poo.

Wanting to post things down the toilet is a relatively common practice for many children with autism! This illustrates the lack of understanding of what toilets are for.

Difficulty in coping with change

We know that most children with autism find change very difficult. This can include changing from nappies to pants or using the toilet instead of a nappy; they have often learned that nappies are familiar and more comfortable. Pants can give very different sensations, especially if they are wet or soiled, while modern absorbent nappies reduce a child's sensation of wetness. Children with autism frequently prefer to keep to the routine they are used to, and they can be very reluctant and resistant to doing things differently.

As well as different clothes, children have to get used to different routines, including using the bathroom and toilet and the sounds and smells of these places. They also have to get used to different messages and expectations from their parents and carers.

Sensory differences

What we see, hear, feel, smell and taste gives us information about our environment and ourselves. It helps us make sense of the world and enables us to act appropriately within it.

Many children with autism can experience some form of sensory sensitivity (Klintwall *et al.* 2010 ; Smith-Myles 2001). This can occur in one or more of the seven senses – sight, sound, smell, touch, taste, balance and body awareness. A person's senses are either intensified (hypersensitive) or reduced (hyposensitive) and these factors often impact upon a child's ability to learn to use the toilet. The bathroom is often a place that the child finds challenging to enter. It can be visually overwhelming for some children, with bright colours or lighting, a different type of flooring, strong smells and perfumes, all of which can potentially cause anxiety, confusion or distraction from the task you are trying to teach them. Alternatively, for other children it could be a place of sensory stimulation and fun; and the enjoyment of these experiences will often take priority for the child above learning to use the toilet to wee and poo.

Chapter 13 will explore these sensory differences in more detail, describing the impact they can have and considering possible solutions.

Understanding the autism spectrum

There have been different views about the variety of presentations and labels for conditions related to autism, including discussion about their inclusion on the autism spectrum.

Lorna Wing[2] has written to clarify the use of terminology and diagnostic labels to describe the different patterns of disabilities found on the autism spectrum. She has discussed some of the different terms used for autism spectrum disorder and the labels sometimes used for particular patterns of disabilities found among people with autism, including non-verbal learning disorder or semantic-pragmatic disorder. She includes Pathological Demand Avoidance syndrome (PDA) and feels that this is best understood as part of the autism spectrum.

Pathological Demand Avoidance syndrome (PDA)

The PDA Society explains that children with PDA will avoid demands made by others, due to their high anxiety levels when they feel that they are not in control.[3] This was first described by Professor Elizabeth Newson to describe a group of children seen that were atypical of the clinical picture of autism but who had a resemblance to each other. It is now increasingly recognised as part of the autism spectrum.

There is now a reference book for clinicians,[4] which can provide further information on both diagnosing PDA and supportive strategies. Children with this condition avoid compliance and may need a different approach (see Chapter 16).

Associated conditions

Other specific developmental disorders frequently coexist in children with autism, and these affect strategies needed to help learn toileting skills. These include Attention Deficit Disorder, with or without hyperactivity (ADD or ADHD), coordination difficulties and other specific learning difficulties.

---

2   www.autism.org.uk/about-autism/all-about-diagnosis

3   www.pdasociety.org.uk

4   www.pdasociety.org.uk/resources/awareness-matters-booklet

Eating and drinking patterns in children with autism

Many children with autism have restricted eating and drinking patterns, linked to rigidity and accepting change. Sensory sensitivities linked to texture and taste can play a key part in restricting the range of foods accepted or enjoyed by children with autism. These eating patterns can have physical effects on bowel and bladder function, including constipation, loose stools and bladder frequency. This illustrates the importance of considering the contribution of both physical factors and how autism may affect their understanding and learning.

Physical development

The functioning of the bowel and bladder is complicated, and many children have difficulties in learning bowel and bladder control. This may be linked to problems with bowel and bladder activity, constipation, bowel intolerances and bladder conditions such as bladder immaturity. These factors need to be assessed and managed as part of the strategy for developing continence. A child's awareness of bowel and bladder function varies between individuals, and develops as a child grows older. Problems with bowel and bladder functioning is a fairly common condition in many children, and may need to be considered and evaluated to help in deciding the best way to help a child with autism to learn toileting skills.

It is important not to assume that a delay in toileting is always due to the child's autism.

Stress and anxiety

Many children with autism can experience high levels of stress and anxiety, often linked to their struggle to understand the world around them. This can make it difficult to process language and learn new skills. It can lead to a child exhibiting distressed behaviours and an increased need for routine.

Many children can develop fears and anxiety about using the toilet, and can imagine things lurking down it. This may be influenced by adverts they see, for example those for cleaning products which suggest that germ monsters live around the toilet seat!

Timing of toilet training

It is best not to postpone toilet training too long if possible. It is useful to remember that children are learning all the time, and they may be learning that wee and poo goes in a nappy. Parents can also be misinformed by friends and professionals to leave toileting until the child is older. While this at times may be best for some children and families, it may make later learning more difficult.

The timing of the autism diagnosis may also vary. If this is delayed, both professionals and parents may not understand the difficulties that learning toileting skills may present.

PART 2

PREPARATION AND PLANNING

Chapter 4

CHOOSING THE RIGHT TIME

Getting the timing right of any new toilet training plan is essential. This applies both for teaching initial toilet training skills or attempting to understand and make changes to behaviour. The physiological signs of readiness for toilet training are important to evaluate, but there are several other aspects that are important to think about carefully.

When a child is four years old, if toileting has not been commenced, it is important to make a plan. For older children, it is never too late to start teaching toileting skills, and the timing for these children will have different factors to consider.

It is important to consider the child's needs and those of the parents or carers, and to look at what else might be going on in their lives that may affect the learning of a new skill. Although all children are different, there are nearly always some steps that will help to begin or develop the learning process.

Is it the right time for the child?
Many children with autism will be upset by changes in routine, and often try to keep things consistent and avoid change. Toilet training is going to involve many different things that may challenge a child, so it is helpful to look at other changes that might be affecting them.

These may include new settings, skills and routines, and anxiety linked to these should be assessed.

The right time for introducing change will be different for each child.

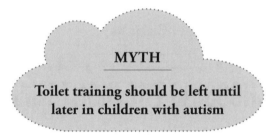

MYTH

Toilet training should be left until later in children with autism

New class, school or age

Some children respond well to changes in their routine linked to something more concrete, such as changing class, school or a birthday. This can be facilitated by good planning, preparation and ongoing support for the child.

'Now I'm seven, I will use the toilet to wee in.'

Some children may associate certain behaviours with certain settings, so the concept of 'new place, new rules' can be a vital teaching opportunity for these children. Setting the rules on the first day in a new setting may make sense to them. Preparation for this is vital.

Other children may find changes to their routine, such as a new class or school, very difficult to manage, and may need increased support before adding further changes.

Behaviour

If a child is displaying distressed or challenging behaviours, it is essential to focus on understanding and responding to these. It may be necessary to address the child's distress, and plan for later intervention to address the toileting issues.

Difficulty with behaviour may make learning to use the toilet difficult, but does not necessarily mean that all aspects of toileting should be postponed. It will need to be considered in deciding which next step is appropriate, and maybe this will have to be less challenging, and more difficult steps postponed until a better time. Behaviours, often caused by sensory overload or distress, that include physically challenging behaviours or meltdowns (where all control is lost) may need to be evaluated first.

Careful analysis of behaviour is discussed in Chapter 14 and this will help in deciding timing, strategies and priorities for intervention.

Stress and anxiety

It is often easier to introduce changes at a time when a child is fairly settled and to avoid times of severe anxiety. If a child is feeling calm, they are more likely to be able to process information and learn new skills. Sympathetic support and understanding will always facilitate learning. In the next chapter we discuss ways to reduce stress and anxiety as this can be an important step in addressing toileting difficulties.

Is it the right time for the adults involved?

Success will be increased if the timing for teaching to use the toilet is done at the right time for parents and others caring for the child. It is always difficult to be a parent, especially of a child with additional needs. Parents themselves may have other problems that also need to be considered, including health, employment, income and education. Although it is always best to start toilet training as soon as practicable, it is important to try to do it at a time that works for the adults involved. These will include parents and other adults that support the child, including carers, grandparents, staff at school, out-of-school services, and during short breaks and in residential settings. If toilet training is stressful for adults, this can give negative messages to the child and create more difficulty.

Have there been changes in family circumstances?

Changes such as a new baby, new house and new childcare arrangements can all require adjustments and may cause stress for the family, and therefore could affect decisions about how and when to begin a toileting plan. It is always helpful to spend time exploring the family dynamics in deciding the best time to start addressing this and consider the time and energy that may be required.

Have there been changes for staff?

Staff support and workload are relevant in assessing ways a child needs to be supported. Changes to staff and teams happen frequently and their needs may be relevant in deciding the support a child will need in an education or care setting. Both children and staff may need time to adjust to any changes and develop relaxed, constructive relationships.

Is everyone emotionally ready?

Attempting to understand, change or teach any behaviour can be stressful for all, which is why it is vital to ensure everyone is emotionally ready to cope with this, in order to communicate effectively with each other and maintain consistency.

'I had to do it when the time was right for me.' *(Mother of a nine-year-old)*

Is there a good network of support?

Effective support is essential for everyone. Many people find it very helpful to talk to someone else about how they are feeling, and about the progress they are, or are not, making. This will help in overcoming any challenges and frustrations that arise. Support may be obtained from parent groups, autism teams and education or health staff.

Postponing toilet training

There are many different aspects of learning that may be started as preparation to give the child messages and skills as a basis for toilet training. If the time is really not right for the child, the family or others supporting them, it may be agreed that it is best to postpone initiating a toileting programme. If this is necessary, it is important to be clear about the reasons for this and agree a date to review it.

TOP TIPS

1. Think about the right time to start toilet training for the child and the family.

2. Don't keep putting it off!

3. Consider emotional readiness.

4. Ensure a good support network is in place.

5. Make sure everyone is involved and can be consistent.

Chapter 5

FIRST STEPS

PREPARATION FOR TOILET TRAINING

It is important to ensure that the foundations are in place to make toilet training more successful and less problematic. Good preparation is needed to help children learn any stage of toilet training or associated skills.

These early stages can be a relatively easy way to introduce some of the initial ideas and skills to children that can be utilised later in successful toilet training. Preparation can be started early and it is never too soon to do this. Many caregivers can become focused and frustrated with children coming out of nappies and sitting on the toilet, and if there is inadequate preparation before this stage then these skills will be much harder to teach.

MYTH

Toilet training means taking the nappy away

Children often have different starting points and different challenges in understanding how to use the toilet. This could be learning to go into the bathroom for one child, getting used to wearing different clothes for another, or deciding on what communication is needed for yet another.

There are many steps that parents and carers need to put in place before starting formal toilet training. For children with autism, there are many simple things that may need to be specifically taught, that other children naturally pick up, such as what toilets are for. This can be a way of introducing toilet training, making it fun, and starting with small easy steps in a relaxed way.

Preparation also involves ensuring that all the adults are communicating and working together cooperatively and regularly reviewing the child's progress and the next target to aim for.

Learning to use the toilet is like going from the bottom to the top of the stairs – you can't jump straight there, you have to go step by step!

When supporting a child with any aspect of learning to use the toilet, it is always helpful to agree an action plan to support a step-by-step approach and consider the next goal.

There are various factors that may need to be taken into account, and not everything may be relevant to every child:

Toilet team – everyone who needs to be involved

Toilet talk – words, symbols, signs, objects of reference or pictures

Toilet awareness – of being wet and soiled

Toilet territory – learning what toilets are for

Toilet techniques – clothing and nappies

Toilet technicalities – seating, rails, stools, timers…

Toilet teaching – learning to sit on the toilet

Toilet timetabling – learning to manage change

Toilet tensions – impact of stress on learning new skills.

Toilet team!

Every team needs a leader! The leader needs to inspire, coordinate, and if necessary identify any difficulties people are having with following the agreed plan.

It is important to have everyone involved in creating the plan and following it consistently. This includes using the same words, objects, cues and routines as agreed. There need to be regular reviews of progress, and modifications made where needed.

Sometimes the stages may be very small, such as gradually taking more steps into the bathroom! These are important components that can be built on.

> One family told how they used to hold monthly 'poo meetings' to enable everyone involved to discuss how they were progressing with the programme, and to share any successes or concerns with each other.

Regular contact between team members can prevent the child becoming confused and stressed, and will promote a successful outcome.

> A group of staff who worked in different settings were discussing how best to help a child they all supported. It soon became clear that each setting was doing something different, which appeared to be causing confusion for the child.

As part of the preparation programme, the team involved may need opportunity to develop their understanding of either autism or toilet training. This might include specific training if necessary.

Toilet talk!

The specific difficulties with communication in children with autism can contribute to delays in learning complicated skills such as using the toilet.

Clear and consistent communication is essential for helping and supporting children to understand what they are being asked to do.

Words

Choose and agree the words that are going to be used for all aspects of learning toilet skills, and ensure that everyone uses these consistently. This is one of the most important things that the toilet team need to have in place. These are the essential words it is important to agree – different families and cultures may use different words and expressions:

- Toilet (the thing you sit on!)

- Bathroom (the room where the toilet is!)

- Toilet paper or wipes

- Clothing (is everyone using the same words for items of clothing?)

- Urine, wee, pee, etc.

- Faeces, poo, poop, etc.

- Bottom

- Penis

- Anus.

The non-verbal aspects of talking about wee and poo, including tone and volume of voice, facial expressions and gestures, are important to consider, and unless used consistently may give the child different messages.

Language

This needs to be appropriate for the child's understanding, and input from a speech and language therapist can be extremely valuable. Some children will only understand and respond to single words, while others may communicate in simple sentences. A clear principle for children with autism is to use fewer but more meaningful words.

How sentences are phrased can affect understanding. Giving positive instructions such as 'It's time to go to the toilet' or 'It's wee time' can be more meaningful to a child. If we ask 'Do you want to go to the toilet?' the reply may well just be 'No'. Why would they want to do that, when they do not understand, do not like it or find it very scary!

Visual information

Many children with autism may find it easier to understand and process visual information. Visual supports can include objects of reference, signs, symbols, pictures or photographs. There are some specific communication systems that a child may already be familiar with such as Picture Exchange Communication System (PECS) or specific resources such as Widget or Do2Learn (see the Resources section at the back of this book).

Preparation may need to include agreement about which visual supports or objects of reference to use. These should also include the words or phrases to remind everyone involved what to say.

The type of visual supports should match the child's level of understanding and interest. Pictures, symbols or photos should be chosen to help the child learn what they are being asked to do. Sometimes it may be helpful to include an image or design background of something the child is particularly interested in to engage their focus.

My son has R2D2 from Star Wars in the corner of all his visual prompts!

The resource *Toilet Time*[5] has a range of pictures that can be used with boys or girls and help them understand and learn different aspects of the toileting process. The resource *One Step at a Time*[6] includes a range of symbols showing children the steps in the toileting process, and can be chosen by parents as appropriate.

At times, children may enjoy and learn from a more literal image of what needs to go in the toilet. Dolls that are able to 'pee and poo' in the toilet may be useful to show some children what happens.

---

5   www.sensetoys.com

6   www.continencevictoria.org.au/resources/one-step-time-parents-guide-toilet-skills-children-special-needs

'I bought a doll from the charity shop, and was able to make it wee and poo in the toilet using diluted orange and mashed potato and gravy granules!' *(Mother of child with autism)*

There is a range of cartoons and books for children that illustrate clearly wee and poo going into the toilet and what happens to it. Bookshops and YouTube may be useful places to search for these.

Children may need visual supports introduced gradually, with help to understand the words that relate to them and the activities they describe. Putting or showing the visual support by the action or place it shows may help the child to understand. The pictures or symbols can be gradually combined into short sequences of actions, to help the child know what comes next.

Toilet awareness!

Some children who still wear nappies will often have no awareness of feeling wet or soiled. Most disposable nappies nowadays are so absorbent that they ensure that there is no moisture in contact with the skin, so the child does not receive any physical sensation that they are wet. Children wearing washable nappies may experience a greater sensation of feeling wet or soiled. A child's awareness of touch sensation may be linked to sensory differences (discussed in Chapter 13).

If you think a child has little appreciation of being wet or soiled, the following things may be helpful:

- Nappy liner inside the nappy

- A piece of kitchen roll inside the nappy

- Pants worn inside the nappy

- Going without a nappy or pants on sunny days in the garden

- Starting to wear pants for a short time in the day; this time could be gradually increased.

Toilet territory!

Many children may not have learnt what toilets and bathrooms are for. If they are still in nappies they may often have been changed elsewhere, such as their bedroom or the living room at home, or in a side-room or medical room at school. They may have little idea that wee and poo are supposed to go down the toilet if their only experience is of having their nappy changed. They may not have seen other people use the toilet, and if they have, they may not relate it to themselves.

Things that may help a child understand where wee and poo should go include:

- Always change their nappy in the bathroom if possible. This can help a child learn that toilet activity takes place there. Keep everything needed for dealing with wee and poo in the bathroom to give consistent messages.

- Show the child how the poo is emptied from the nappy into the toilet. This can help a child learn where poo is supposed to go, and sometimes they may be able to help, flushing the toilet or waving poo goodbye.

- Some families have an 'open door' policy on the bathroom, so the child can see other people using the toilet. This can be a useful part of preparation for some children, although some children with autism may have difficulty applying behaviours they see in others to themselves.

Toilet techniques!

The ultimate aim of any toilet training programme is to teach a child to be as independent as their abilities allow.

It is important to plan and think about the clothing that will be easy for them to take on and off when needed.

A starting point may be getting used to wearing different clothes. It may take time for some children to get used to wearing trousers and learn to undo them and pull them down. Girls may need to get used to wearing skirts and lifting them up.

Some children may need be taught undressing and dressing skills, including physically putting a hand over theirs to help to show them the movements needed.

Backwards chaining as a means of teaching this can be helpful. This involves breaking down the steps of a task and teaching them in reverse order, thus giving the child the experience of success and completion with every attempt. In practice, this involves getting the child to complete the last part of a task themselves, and then work backwards, so they complete a little bit more of the task each time:

- Stage 1 – pull up trousers as far as their hips, they do the last little bit

- Stage 2 – pull up trousers halfway up the thighs, they do the rest

- Stage 3 – pull up trousers just above the knees, they do the rest

- etc...

This approach is great for building their self-esteem, as they always get the sense of completion from finishing the task. Hooray!!!!!

Chapter 13 will discuss some specific sensory reasons why they might feel comfortable in nappies. Part of the preparation for children who need to feel the increased pressure that they have become used to might include introducing tightly fitting pants or shorts to help replace this feeling.

Toilet technicalities!

Preparation involves examining the bathroom environment and considering whether any additional equipment, products, activities or rewards are needed.

An environmental audit of the bathrooms that they will be using can help with this. An example is provided in the Practical Tools section.

Interventions could include reducing glare from lighting and creating a less cluttered and peaceful environment.

An environmental audit can also provide an indication of the supplies that might be needed, for example rails for stability or a footstool for good positioning. It is important to have all the necessary equipment in place before starting the toilet training programme or trying to change a particular behaviour.

Suggested requirements are:

- *Visual supports* (see above).

- *Pants.* A good supply of pants that the child will accept. Some will like those with a favourite character on them, although there are some that might find this very distracting, and might be concerned that Thomas the Tank Engine may get wet! These children may prefer plain ones. Consider the sensory feeling of these, including type of fabric and presence of labels.

- *Tight pants or shorts.* To provide the child with firm pressure if they have a need for this sensory input.

- *Toilet seats.* It is essential that a child feels completely secure on the toilet. The type of seat needs to be the right size for the child so they feel safe. Specific children's seats are available in many stores. It is useful to consider a model that is less likely to need changes in future. Some children may be sensitive to the temperature and sensation of the seat, so the option of a padded seat or one with changeable fabric may be useful.

  Toilet seats should fit properly and not move as this may cause anxiety and be very upsetting. Children often worry that they may fall down the toilet, even if this is unlikely to happen. Seats can be made more stable with foam beneath the ring.

- *Portable toilet seat.* Some children may benefit from having a portable seat they are familiar with which they can take with them to help use other toilets. This can help them feel safe and comfortable on the toilet and supports them with making the transition from using the toilet at home to others.

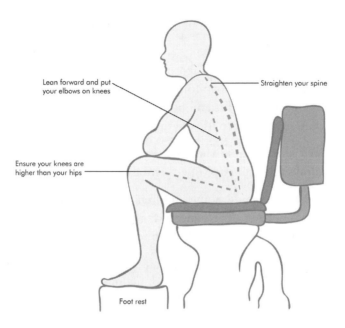

Correction position for using the toilet

- *Footstool.* These are always good and help with balance and body positioning. When a child sits on the toilet they often need to have their feet resting on a flat and firm surface. If they cannot reach the floor to do this, they can feel unsteady. Many parents have made satisfactory home-made versions from boxes!

- *Hand rails.* These may be needed for children with balance difficulties. The Occupational Therapy team may give advice about relevant adaptations.

- *Back support.* Some children may benefit from having something firm behind them to help them feel balanced, stable and to know where their body is. Items such as a rolled up towel or part of a foam swim tube at the back of the toilet seat can help with this.

- *Commodes.* These may be a useful option for those children with physical difficulties or mobility problems, or in some situations where use of the toilet or bathroom is highly problematic.

- *Lighting.* Some children find that bright lights used in bathrooms are uncomfortable and overwhelming. The use of lower voltage lights and bulbs may be better, particularly for those who need to use the toilet in the night.

- *Wet wipes.* These can give increased tactile feedback for children learning to wipe themselves.

- *Disposable gloves.* Some children may be extremely anxious about putting their hand near their bottom and disposable gloves for the child could help reduce this concern.

- *Timers.* These can be invaluable when teaching a child to sit on the toilet. They can show how long to sit there, and this can be gradually increased. Visual timers, such as sand timers or the Time Timer™, which show time moving without the need to be able to tell the time, can be helpful.

- *Interesting and distracting activities.* For many children, sitting on the toilet is really boring! The provision of a selection of washable toys or books that are only used in the bathroom can help with making it a more interesting and friendly place to be. Sensory fiddle toys, such as soft balls, tangle toys or bubbles to blow, may provide sensory input and enjoyment. An interesting picture or cartoon on the wall at the child's eye level, or a spinning toy that hangs from the ceiling, might help them relax and give them something to focus on.

Toilet teaching!

Many children need to build up confidence in feeling comfortable sitting on the toilet. This is best started simply for a very short time, and then gradually increasing the duration. Children should not be encouraged to stay on the toilet for too long. Anything over five minutes may teach them that toilets are boring or that people just sit on toilets! The time sitting on the toilet should be adjusted for the age and concentration level of the child (five minutes is still too long for very young children).

Good practice would be:

- Establish between six and eight practice times a day; plan this with all involved and put it onto the daily timetable (many children will have a visual timetable). Timetabling this will give it the equal priority it needs alongside other activities.

- Link the practice times to cues in the child's daytime routine, for example playtime or mealtime.

- Choose something the child likes to use as a small reward or a motivator to maintain their interest.

- Sit the child on the toilet, using a visual timer to indicate when to get off. The first few sessions may be just a few seconds long, and this can be gradually increased as the child learns to achieve this skill.

- Remember that the aim of the sessions is about getting the child used to sitting on the toilet and to be comfortable and relaxed. It is not yet about getting them to wee or poo in the toilet.

- If they do happen to wee or poo in the toilet during a practice session (and sometimes they do!), then the session should be ended and an additional reward or praise for the achievement given.

Toilet timetabling!

Toilet training often involves a change in routine for a child. Preparation may need to involve getting a child used to changes.

Good practice for introducing change would be:

- Make life as consistent and predictable as possible for the child so as to reduce their level of anxiety.

- Gradually introduce small changes into their routine, with the reassuring message that other things will still take place.

- Develop a Social Story™ about why things are going to be different. Social stories are ways to help people with autism develop social understanding. Developed by Carol Gray in 1991, the goal of a social story is to share accurate social information in a way that is easily understood by the child. It can include reassurance about things that will stay the same. Sample social stories are in the Practical Tools section.

One benefit of disliking change is that when a good toileting routine is established, a child may like this to be maintained!

Toilet tensions

Some children with autism might be scared of crocodiles down the toilet!

Many children are frightened of toilets and some may think of scary things lurking at the bottom such as snakes, crocodiles and germ monsters. These ideas may originate from cartoons they have seen or adverts for cleaning products.

Many children with autism find life very stressful and attention to this is a key factor to consider when toilet training. The initial starting point for some may need to focus on reducing their level of stress and anxiety. Andrew Powell (2011) discusses general principles for reducing anger, anxiety and distressed behaviour in the book *Autism: Understanding and Managing Anger*. He suggests:

- Reduce confrontation

- Provide reassurance

- Communicate clearly – using fewer but better chosen words

- Create structure – give the child a consistent routine

- Consider sensory needs.

Many children will benefit from having clear structure to their days. This will include teaching them to follow sequences, and these can then be used in future toilet training or learning related skills.

There may be other difficulties, such as challenging behaviour, which may need further input prior to implementing a toilet training plan.

Chapter 6

TOILET READINESS

For children over four, toileting should take priority over other skills.

Assessment of toilet readiness includes an evaluation of the child's development, awareness and understanding, together with the maturation of bowel and bladder function. It is a useful guide to helping decide if a child is ready to begin toilet training, and if this is likely to be successful. The Royal College of Nursing (2006) has published a care pathway and this emphasises the importance of promoting continence and a full assessment of a child's continence needs and toilet training skills.

In thinking about toilet readiness we try to assess a child's ability to understand and learn new skills, their awareness of the way their bodies are working, and also how the bladder and bowel are maturing.

For children with delays in understanding and learning, the bowel and bladder can physically mature and develop control at a rate similar to other children.

It is important to start a toileting plan early. Maria Wheeler (1998) emphasises this and says that once a person is beyond four years old toilet training should become a priority. If starting toilet training is delayed it can make acquiring the skill more difficult later.

Clear indications of toilet readiness

Occasionally children may clearly indicate they are aware that they are wet or soiled and want to have their nappy changed, perhaps by trying to remove clothes or bringing a new nappy to be put on. This clearly shows that the child is aware of bowel or bladder activity and understands that this is associated with putting on a clean nappy. The ability to remain clean and dry through the night is another less common indication of toilet readiness.

Awareness of bladder and bowel function

It is important to be aware of any cues a child gives about their awareness of bowel and bladder control, and the use of toilets. At times these may be quite subtle and not apparent unless looked for carefully. Although a child may not verbalise, they may indicate when they are wet or soiled, sometimes by trying to remove a nappy. They may go quiet and still when emptying the bowel or bladder, and sometimes go to a particular place to do this, such as behind the sofa. This will suggest that not only is a child aware of bowel and bladder activity, but they are able to take some action to be in a chosen place for this, although this is often not the place a parent would choose!

Some children may show interest in toilets or indicate they are aware of others using the toilet to empty their bowels and bladder.

Bladder development

It is very helpful to evaluate the bladder function in order to know when to start toilet training, and this also helps with planning a programme. This is usually done by assessing how long a child can go before emptying their bladder. Modern nappies have great absorbency so the layer next to the child's skin does not feel wet, and this reduces the opportunity to learn about the sensations associated with bladder emptying. The ability to hold the urine for one to two hours is a sign that the bladder is developing maturity, and is storing a normal volume of urine before emptying.

This is often evaluated by a baseline toileting assessment to keep a record of the frequency of bladder emptying. It may be done by using trainer pants or kitchen roll under a nappy and checking it regularly (at least every hour). Sometimes children may be happy to experiment without nappies at all (in fine weather!) or wearing normal pants. Parents will often have knowledge of which way will be least stressful both for their child and the family. Do a baseline assessment for a few days to gain an understanding of the child's bladder pattern, which may vary depending on the time of day and fluid intake. It is helpful to record this on a chart, and it is important to discuss this and include observations of others who look after the child. A sample chart is given at the end of this chapter, with a more complete version provided in the Practical Tools section.

Sometimes, especially for older children, wearing an electronic alarm with a moisture sensor that rings or vibrates when the child is wet may be useful to monitor how often the bladder is emptying.

If parents know how often the bladder empties it may not be necessary to do a formal recording, as this information may enough to decide how to toilet train.

Another indicator for the ability to develop bladder control may the ability to stay dry during naps.

It is useful to consider the fluid intake. For good bladder function, and to develop awareness, it is helpful to have a good intake of clear watery fluids over the day. Usually seven drinks a day or 1000–1400ml is suggested (NICE 2012, Guideline 111). This keeps the urine reasonably dilute and helps to promote bladder filling. Inadequate fluid intake can make the urine become concentrated, which can irritate the bladder. Constant drinking can also increase the urine output and cause more frequent bladder emptying. Recording fluid intake can be helpful in deciding future action.

A delay in the ability to hold the urine for longer periods can suggest that the bladder is not developing the ability to function efficiently. This can be discussed with a health professional, and it may be appropriate to consider whether this is just immaturity or if there should be further evaluation or investigations of bladder function. Factors such as fluid intake and constipation may affect bladder filling and emptying, so may need to be evaluated.

Bowel development

As well as the bladder pattern, the bowel activity and frequency should also be recorded. It is useful to note the amount, size and consistency of the poo as well as the frequency of bowel action. A normally functioning bowel will produce formed, fairly soft bowel movements that are comfortable to pass. A normal bowel pattern varies from several times a day to every two or three days. It can be affected by diet and fluid intake. If the large bowel is not emptying fully, it may press on the bladder causing more frequent bladder emptying, and therefore make training more difficult.

Many children, including those with autism, have rigid, unusual eating patterns that may affect the regularity of bowel action. Constipation in these children occurs frequently, and may need to be treated before starting a toileting plan.

Mental age and understanding

This can be difficult to assess in young children with autism, and not all children will yet have had a diagnosis. Some children will have had a formal assessment of their cognitive levels, and a mental age of two of more would suggest a level of understanding where they are able to be toilet trained. However, it can be difficult at times to test cognitive understanding in children with autism, and their profile can be uneven.

A child's communication skills, including their appreciation of language or signs, may give an indication of their ability to understand words and simple instructions or follow commands. These may need to be linked to visual cues to reinforce understanding. An assessment of communication is often done by a speech and language therapist and this may be helpful in deciding if toilet training is appropriate, and how to help a child learn how to do it.

The ability to learn other skills such as getting dressed and undressed, and constructive play, may give some indication about a child's understanding. It can be useful to observe the child's level of interest in the activities of others and their ability to begin to imitate some of the behaviours they observe.

Motor development

The ability to become toilet trained may be affected by motor skills and balance, including the ability to sit securely on a toilet or potty. If this is difficult, there may be a need to consider equipment that will support the child securely. Any difficulty with fine motor skills will affect a child's ability to manage clothes.

Autism factors

- Communication and understanding of language, words and pictures or symbols is important to tell children what is expected, and why they should try to learn to use the toilet. Their communication skills will indicate if they can learn the skill, and also influence the strategies that can be used for toilet training.

- Sensory differences are very common, either hyper- (increased) or hypo- (reduced) reactions to sensations, and these may affect the way a child with autism is able to engage in toileting.

- Sequential learning and the ability to establish sequences and adding actions into a routine will affect the way in which toileting may be introduced.

- The presence of routines and rituals may affect a child's ability to accept changes and new routines in toilet training.

- Rigidity will indicate how the child will respond to the introduction of new strategies.

- Levels of stress should be considered and will affect the need to pace toilet training and provide input to help with the reduction of anxiety.

- Generalisation of skills to new situations and the ability to do this should be considered.

Emotional needs

The child's emotional needs and behaviour should be considered both in decisions about embarking on toileting and in how it should be undertaken. This does not suggest that toilet training should not be started, but the pace and targets may need to be adjusted to be appropriate for the child's needs.

Parental readiness

Toilet training is a cooperative process, so if for any reason parents are not ready to undertake this, it may need to be postponed. If the parents are not ready to start toilet training (and this is very common), postponement needs to be considered without guilt. Parental stress will have a great impact on how successful toilet training is likely to be. This is an essential consideration, as parents often have to cope with many other stressful aspects of bringing up a child with autism, including coming to terms with the diagnosis. They also have to negotiate with many professionals and authorities and appointments in meeting their child's and family's needs.

The needs of other family members, including siblings and sometimes elderly grandparents, may need to be considered.

Assessing for toilet readiness

A sample from the chart for assessing a child's readiness for toilet training is provided at the end of this chapter, together with a sample behavioural assessment chart. (See the Practical Tools section at the back of the book for the complete downloadable versions.)

Some important things to remember about a toileting readiness assessment are:

- It can be useful to do this as a team approach with parents and others who know the child well.

- All the separate areas need to be considered.

- It can be used as the basis for developing a practical toilet plan.

- It does not exclude starting some preparation strategies for toilet training.

- All children change, so it should be reviewed regularly.

- Sometimes instinct can also give a guide about a child's ability, and children sometimes surprise adults with their ability to learn things.

If it is felt that the assessment indicates a child is not ready for toilet training, it is important that everyone responsible for the child is aware of the reasons for this, and agrees how and when to revisit this issue. There should be an agreed plan to start toilet training in the future, with time scales.

Sample Bowel and Bladder Recording Chart

See the Practical Tools section for the complete format.

	Day 1	Day 2	Day 3	Day 4	Day 5	Day 6	Day 7
Date							
Time	Wet Dry Soiled	Wet Dry Soiled	Wet Dry Soiled	Wet Dry Soiled	Wet Dry Soiled	Wet Dry Soiled	Wet Dry Soiled
7.00 7.30							
8.00 8.30							
9.00 9.30							
Cont...							

Sample Toilet Readiness Assessment

See the Practical Tools section for the complete form.

	Always	Often	Occasionally	Never
Understanding				
Understands visual cues and/or objects of reference				
Verbal language				
Response to commands				
Motor skills				
Reliable balance				
Accurate fine motor ability				

	Always	Often	Occasionally	Never
Awareness				
Indicates bowel or bladder activity				
Empties bowel or bladder in a selected place				
Shows interest in others using the toilet				
Bladder maturity				
Able to hold wee for 1–2 hours				
Dry during daytime naps				
Dry nappies at night				
Bowel functioning				
Regular bowel pattern				
Presence of constipation				
Presence of diarrhoea or loose bowels				

Sample Behavioural Assessment

See the Practical Tools section for the complete form.

Behaviours	Present	Intermittent	Absent
Anxiety			
Rigid behaviour			
Sensory difficulties			
Routines and rituals			
Ability to transfer skills to other situations			
Ability to understand sequences of activities			
Good understanding of words or symbols			
Behaviour – anger and meltdowns			
Behaviour – withdrawal			

Chapter 7

DEVELOPING A TOILETING PLAN

The 'toileting Olympics'

'We did the toileting Olympics in the first week of the summer holiday, with races to the toilet and homemade medals for winning against the wee and for beating the record. After this it was much better, although we still had further to go. She now had a clear idea of what we were aiming for and we had had great fun together.' *(Mother of a six-year-old)*

The important thing is to make it simple, fun and achievable, with small steps, but keep moving forward. It is like climbing a steep hill. It is necessary to decide the route, look at the weather forecast, and arrange the best time to start. It is often necessary to climb gradually, but you need to keep moving forward to get to the top. You may want to stop at times to have a rest, to enjoy the view and to see how far you have come. You need to keep your expedition together and keep going steadily to get to the top. When you get there, it is exciting and there is great satisfaction for everyone. Afterwards you can decide which hill you are going to climb next!

It is always important to have a clear plan of action. This needs clear goals and good strategies. In deciding these it is often a good idea to consult people who know the child well and also consider information and tips from other parents, professionals and online resources.

Children and families may have different starting points, and the challenges will be different. It is often helpful to break the task into achievable steps and not to try to do everything at once. For some children it may be helpful at the beginning to focus toilet training on a convenient part of a day, such as an hour in the morning or after school, and then gradually increase the time.

There is no right way to begin, and it doesn't necessarily need to be at the beginning. It can sometimes be good to start on the easiest and most achievable step, to have success for everyone to build on. It may be necessary to spend time on each stage; however, often children do the unexpected, and surprise everyone.

Advice and support

Advice and support is important for parents and carers, and helps to provide confidence and reduce stress. It may be available from continence nurses, health visitors, school and children's nurses. Many other professionals working with children and families may also have information, advice and resources. Parents often receive help and advice from children's groups, parent groups and blogs. There are specialist continence clinics in some areas and details of these should be available from key workers and other professionals. ERIC has details of continence services available in most areas of the UK. We include details of resources, books and leaflets in the Resources section at the end of the book.

Toileting routines

Many children with autism like routines, and these can be utilised in toilet training programmes:

- Choose the timing of toilet trips based on what the toileting assessment found was their usual pattern of emptying their bladder. Try to link toilet times to predictable events in the day such as meal or play times. Include toileting on visual timetables if they are used.

- Some children may need a route marked to the toilet with arrows, footsteps or coloured tape to remind them of the way.

- A notice on the toilet door may be fun: 'Wee and poo this way.'

- Use positive instructions about using the toilet, such as 'It's time to wee.'

MYTH

When toilet training, you should take a child to the toilet every 30 minutes

Some things to avoid:

- Avoid taking children to the toilet too often. Children will learn that it is boring. It will also not allow the bladder to fill, and this reduces the sensation of a full bladder.

- Don't ask if children want to go to the toilet – the answer is usually 'No' because it is much more fun playing.

- Try to prevent children developing rituals about toileting; these can be more difficult to change if they become established.

If there is lack of progress and everyone decides to give toilet training a rest, make sure there is an agreed time for it to be reattempted. It should never be abandoned indefinitely.

There are many steps needed in learning to use the toilet, some of which are easier than others:

1. Become aware of wee and poo.

2. Recognise the need to go to the toilet.

3. Go to the toilet.

4. Pull down pants.

5. Sit on the toilet.

6. Wee in the toilet.

7. Poo in the toilet.

8. Pull up clothes.

9. Flush toilet.

10. Wash hands.

11. Dry hands.

12. Go and play.

Targets and rewards

These are not bribes, they are motivators! It can be good if children are involved at choosing their targets and rewards, as this helps them to feel involved and in control. However, note that not all children want these.

Targets need to be regularly reviewed and new ones may be needed. This could include increasing the time, for example keeping dry to break-time and then increasing this to lunchtime.

Rewards will also need to be reviewed as children progress in order to maintain improvement. As progress occurs it may be helpful to give a reward symbol, or picture of the reward. This can then be divided in half (or into jigsaw pieces) so the child has to get both halves to receive the reward. When toilet training targets have been successfully achieved, then rewards can be negotiated for new targets.

Rewards and motivators...

- Rewards should be for effort and not just success.

- Rewards should always be for achievable targets, and steps towards success. If you can rarely or never get the reward it rapidly becomes uninteresting.

- Rewards may need to be changed for variety and sustained interest.

- Rewards should not be too big or expensive; this can cause disappointment if the targets are not achieved, and high cost to the purchaser if they are!

Some reward suggestions

- An activity such as playing football or going on the trampoline

- Extra time with a favourite toy, computer game or story time

- Praise, cheers, claps and high fives

- A lucky dip box with small surprises or with notes of nice things to do

- Stars and stickers – special stickers of spacemen or dinosaurs if preferred

- Marbles in a jar with a small prize when the jar is full

- A phone call or text to a grandparent

- A dot to dot of their favourite object, picture or cartoon

- A picture of a toy or game cut up into pieces. The child receives a piece for each success and fits the jigsaw together and gains the reward when it is complete

- A chart with record of a train journey along a track with a station for each success

- A visual graph on the computer

- Sweets, crispy snacks, favourite fruit

- Picture rewards.

'Sam loved frogs, and every time he tried to go the toilet I gave him a picture of a different frog I had cut out. He was delighted to help to choose which one to have.' *(Mother of a four-year-old)*

Note: The amount of any food such as chocolate or sweets given as reward is small, and any worries about this can be offset against the benefits.

Nappies and pants

It is nearly always helpful to change from nappies and pads to pants. This is less confusing, and gives clearer messages about the need to use the toilet. However, it can sometimes take time for the child to get used to the change. Some children may like to choose pants with favourite characters on them. If it is too big a change causing stress, a smaller target time to wear the pants may help, and this can be gradually increased.

Wee or poo first?

Most children find that learning to wee first is easier, because it happens more often so the learning can be more frequent and regular. All children are different, however, and they sometimes get better body messages from a full bowel telling them they need to have a poo. They can also sometimes be more engaged with an activity that happens less often.

Teaching boys to wee – sitting or standing?

The easy answer to this is: whatever works.

It is useful to consider that it might be confusing for boys if they get used to standing to wee in the toilet and then have to learn to sit to poo. It is often best to start with sitting for both to provide consistency, and they can learn to wee standing when they are older. The other advantage of sitting is that children who are standing can run off more easily.

It should be remembered that not all men stand, and different cultures may have differences in toileting etiquette. It may be useful to ask what other men in the family usually do. There are some fun and interesting toilet targets that can be stuck or hung in the toilet for boys to learn how to aim their wee.

Keep the body working well

A good fluid intake is needed to maintain regular full bladder emptying. Monitor the bowel pattern to encourage complete bowel emptying and avoid constipation.

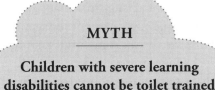

MYTH

Children with severe learning disabilities cannot be toilet trained

Habit training

This describes establishing continence by following a programme of taking the child to the toilet at regular intervals. It is sometimes possible to establish a reliable routine before conscious awareness evolves. This may be particularly relevant for children and young people with severe learning disabilities who are not indicating any bowel or bladder awareness.

Toilet visits should be indicated on a visual timetable. Following successful habit training, the awareness of the need to go to the toilet may develop subsequently. As the child becomes used to being clean and dry they may start to notice if they are wet or soiled (Wheeler 1998).

Consolidation of skills

It is essential to ensure that when a skill towards learning to use the toilet is acquired, then thought is given to consolidation of this. There is sometimes a need to allow time to make sure that the skill is learned and retained reliably. This may be necessary before the next stage. Many children with autism continue to need reminders, prompts or visual cues before managing to initiate the skill themselves.

The need for continued support may be linked to the many other demands upon them, learning other skills, difficulty in remembering sequences of actions, or becoming used to being reminded. It may be advisable to gradually reduce the adult support, encouraging the child to become more independent but ensuring this is not done too quickly. This is an important part of the planning that needs to be in place, reviewed and monitored to ensure that learning is maintained and reduce the likelihood of relapses.

Useful resources

- *One Step at a Time: A Parent's Guide to Toilet Skills for Children with Special Needs,* a structured guide to steps for toileting, with pictures, tips and record charts from PromoCon and www.continencevictoria.org.au/resources/one-step-time-parents-guide-toilet-skills-children-special-needs.

- Visual timers, so the time sitting can be encouraged and extended if needed. These are also available as apps for mobile phones.

- Toilet time flip-book with Velcro-backed pictures to select for individual prompts and sequences from Sense Toys.

- Visual pictures and objects of reference and visual timetables.

- Alarms or vibrating watches to signal when it is time for toileting. These reduce the social interaction so the child may be less likely to challenge this reminder (available from ERIC and other online sources).

- Social Stories™ – these need to be individualised for the child.

TOP TIPS

1. To be successful, learning to use the toilet must be fun.

2. Make sure parents are well supported.

3. Think about the right time to start toilet training for the child and the family.

4. Start sooner rather than later.

5. Break the task up into small achievable targets.

6. Most children will need an individual programme.

7. Think about the advantages in using the toilet, rather than the difficulties.

8. Don't give up, but have a rest if it is difficult.

9. Think about the child's development, physical functioning and autism in planning ways to help in learning to use the toilet.

PART 3

WEE AND POO

MANUFACTURE, STORAGE AND TRANSIT

Chapter 8

THE BLADDER AND HOW IT WORKS

It should never be assumed that problems of bladder control are always linked to a child's autism.

Introduction to bladder problems

Delays and difficulties in bladder control are fairly common problems in young children. These may be linked to a simple delay in developing maturity of bladder function, but bladder control difficulties are also common. These may occur by day, or at night, or both. Although children with physical and learning difficulties, including autism, are more likely to have bowel and bladder problems, it should never be assumed that problems of bladder control are always caused by their autism.

Any child with difficulties in learning bladder control at the usual age will need evaluation and the provision of advice and support for their parents and carers and treatment if required.

Bladder problems in children with autism

It is important to assess both the bladder function and the impact of the child's autism on their bladder awareness and toilet training.

The bladder development is indicated by the ability of the bladder to hold the expected amount of urine for the age of the child.

It is linked to the developing awareness of bladder function and understanding of the need of the bladder to empty. Careful observation of bladder frequency and urine volume will give useful information about how the bladder is working, and recording of the pattern of bladder activity may be helpful.

An assessment of the child's understanding, language and cognitive skills is needed at the same time in order to help evaluate the behavioural aspects of bladder control, and may indicate approaches that will be appropriate. Children with autism may need more help and preparation to understand why and where they are expected to do a wee. They may also need to learn where the wee comes from and why it keeps being produced. Illustrations and stories may be helpful; some of these are included in the Practical Tools section.

Bladder control and developmental delay
Children who have physical and learning difficulties are more likely to have problems with bladder control, and this has been described in a number of studies (Duel *et al.* 2003; Handel *et al.* 2003; Hicks, Carson and Malone 2007; Roijen *et al.* 2001; Van Laecke *et al.* 2001). For any child with a developmental problem there can sometimes be a genetic abnormality, and this is discussed by June Rogers and Mario Patricolo (2014). They point out that wetting difficulties are likely to be linked to the developmental problems and that the possibility of underlying abnormalities should be considered. For any child with a developmental problem there can sometimes be an underlying genetic abnormality. In these children there may be an increased risk of associated structural abnormalities of the urinary system, especially in those with Down's syndrome (Kupferman, Druschel and Kupchick 2009).

Problems with bladder control
There is a range of bladder control problems, and these may affect daytime urine control, night-time control, or both. Poor bladder function may indicate immaturity of bladder development which will resolve with advice and time. However, there may be other underlying difficulties including infection, abnormalities

in development of the urinary system, or problems with bladder emptying. All children with continuing bladder difficulties should have a medical evaluation, including a careful history of their bladder functioning, a physical examination and further investigations if needed.

The structure and functioning of the urinary system

An understanding of bladder function and the development of bladder control is very helpful in developing practical approaches for toilet training. It also helps to identify if there are any problems that may be linked to physical causes.

The urinary system is situated at the lower part of the abdominal cavity and is comprised of the kidneys, ureters, bladder and urethra.

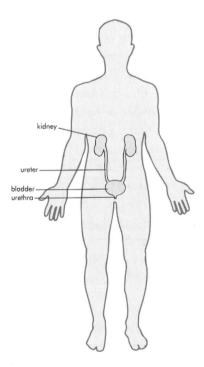

The Urinary System – Kidneys, bladders and tubes

The kidneys are two bean-shaped organs that extract the body's waste products from the blood supply. They are situated at the back of the abdominal cavity on each side of the spine. They contain a complex system of tubules which control the body's salt and fluid balance. The kidneys also regulate the blood pressure, and manufacture hormones. Urine is produced continually and drains down the ureters into the bladder, at a rate of 60ml per hour.

The ureters are tubes on each side of the body between the kidneys and bladder, through which the urine flows to the bladder.

The bladder is situated in the pelvis behind the pubic bone. It is a storage bag with a muscular wall that collects the urine and expands like a balloon as it fills. As urine collects in the bladder, the wall gradually stretches, and when it is nearly full the sensation stimulates the nerves to send messages to the brain which then becomes aware of the full bladder. This is followed by conscious action to control the bladder until going to the toilet. It is important to be aware that as the bladder is filling, little conscious sensation is received and it only becomes a strong sensation when the bladder is full.

The urethra is the tube running from the bladder to the exterior. There are two control muscles or sphincters, one at the bladder outlet, which is under automatic unconscious control, and another at the outlet which is under conscious control.

Bladder emptying is achieved by relaxing the sphincter muscles at the bladder outlet and also at the urethral outlet; at the same time the bladder muscle contracts, forcing the urine to flow out of the bladder. Normally after urination the bladder is fully empty, though sometimes a very small amount of urine remains. As the kidneys continue to produce urine, the bladder starts to fill at once.

Maturation of bladder control

There is a wide variation in the time at which children achieve developmental skills, and bladder control is no exception. It is linked with the bladder's ability to hold increasing amounts of urine before emptying, and the child's awareness of the signals produced by the filling bladder. This is affected by learning opportunities and understanding, as well as motivation and interest. There is also individual variation in development of bladder capacity, and the ability to hold on to the urine. Even young babies store urine in the bladder. Their less mature bladder is not as stable and does not empty efficiently.

As a child grows and develops, the bladder gradually matures and develops a more reliable filling and emptying pattern. The ability to 'hold on' also develops as the child grows up. The normal bladder empties between three and eight times a day.

The average bladder capacity increases as a child grows, and can be calculated as follows: age × 30 + 30 (e.g. at five years of age this will be 5 × 30 + 30 = 180ml). The mature bladder capacity is between 300 and 400ml; this is normally achieved by around ten years of age (Lukacz *et al.* 2011).

For children with autism, their response to bladder development and sensation of a full bladder may be more difficult as some may have reduced awareness of body signals. The awareness of bladder signals may be less intense than those from environmental impulses impinging on their sensation, linked to hearing, vision and body position.

The bladder filling and emptying cycle is shown in the illustration.

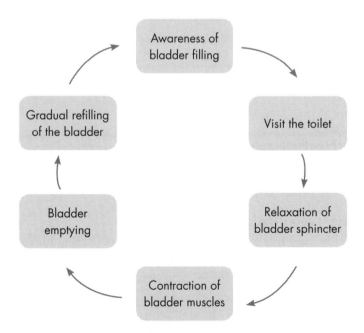

The bladder filling and emptying cycle

Emptying the bladder on demand

Adults and older children are usually able to go to the toilet and pass urine to empty the bladder at convenient times and can anticipate their need to use the toilet. Young children often find this difficult and only gradually learn this skill. They usually learn to go to the toilet when they have the feeling, and of a full bladder. Because there is little sensation until the bladder is full, it can be difficult to learn to wee when it is only partially filled. Most parents have had the experience of asking their young children if they need to do a wee before going out, and are reassured they do not, only to have a panicky message a few minutes later that they need to go urgently!

In addition, young children only gradually develop skills in anticipation and planning as they grow up.

Factors affecting urinary control

- Urinary concentration and fluid intake
- Circadian hormonal control of urine production (vasopressin is a hormone produced by the brain which controls the amount of urine produced and reduces the amount of night-time urine production)
- Body awareness
- Cognitive skills
- Constipation
- Emotional factors and anxiety
- Ability to plan and anticipate.

Urinary concentration and fluid intake

The daily fluid intake as recommended in the NICE guidelines on constipation and bedwetting is 1000–1400ml (about six to seven cups) of clear fluid a day for four- to eight-year-olds. This will vary with the environmental temperature and children's activity level. It can be difficult to do this through a busy day, and many children do not remember, and often do not feel thirsty. Many children, especially those with autism, may only accept particular flavours of drinks. Some children avoid fluids because they think it will help them to avoid going to the toilet at school.

A good fluid intake is necessary for health and good functioning of the bowel and bladder. There is also some evidence that it can affect behaviour and concentration. Children perceive a better sensation from a full bladder with dilute urine. Concentrated urine may irritate the bladder and be more difficult to hold. Water or very dilute drinks are best for hydration and those with high sugar content are not advised.

It can be difficult at times to encourage children to have a good fluid intake, and nagging does not help!

Some things that may help

- Always put a jug of water or other drink on the table at every meal and encourage everyone to have some.

- Many children do not like the taste of water, so drinking dilute drinks they will accept may be a necessary compromise.

- Keep all drinks as dilute as possible.

- Make sure everyone (including parents) drinks regularly at home and at school.

- Have regular drink times with reminders on a timetable, and visual or verbal cues if needed.

- Use corkscrew straws.

- Hold competitions to see who can have the right amount of fluid.

- Provide foods such as soup, salads and jellies which contain quite a lot of fluids.

- Provide ice pops or crushed ice drinks, homemade if possible so there is less sugar.

- Carry out visual experiments of lack of fluids, for example looking at flowers drooping without water.

- Children often like to be scientists – they can check the colour of the wee to see if it is pale yellow. If it is dark yellow or orange it is a sign there is not enough fluid. Colour charts are available from a number of sports websites.[7]

Bladder training

It is often helpful to consider bladder maturity before starting bladder training. Knowing the child's individual bladder emptying pattern and their ability to hold urine is useful for planning. It is always more successful to focus on times when the bladder is likely to be full, as the child will have more sensation, and therefore will do a larger wee which is more satisfying.

As children become toilet trained, they learn to empty their bladder in the toilet, and the awareness of dryness and of feeling the sensation of a full bladder develops from this experience. They may continue to need reminders for some time after learning to wee in the toilet, and the development of their awareness of bladder function will vary.

Bladder control problems in children with autism

Children with autism may have difficulties with bladder control, due to physical functioning, problems linked to their autism and often a combination of both of these. Intervention will need to respond to all the factors contributing to the problems.

Specific difficulties with toilet training in children with autism include:

- Anxiety about new situations, including school and using different toilets, can aggravate any bladder problems.

- Problems with planning and organisation in children may affect toileting programmes and require specific strategies to help.

---

7   For example, www.lotussports.co.uk/Publications/Am%20I%20Hydrated%20
-%20Urine%20Colour%20Chart.pdf.

- Specific concerns about toilets, including sensory differences such as sound and smell, may cause great problems in the ability to go to the toilet.

- Reminders to drink or go to the toilet will need visual reinforcement and literal language used consistently.

- Difficulty in achieving a satisfactory fluid intake is common and can be influenced by reluctance to drink water. Special arrangements may be necessary in school to allow access to other acceptable drinks where appropriate. If needed, specific recommendations can be included as part of reasonable adjustments that are necessary for children with disabilities.

- There may be other needs affecting development, learning and behaviour and it is important to consider these in deciding strategies and priorities.

- Lack of flexibility may create difficulties in using different toilets and transferring skills from home to school or vice versa.

Chapter 9

BLADDER PROBLEMS AND TREATMENT

A range of daytime bladder control difficulties will be discussed in this chapter, including bladder immaturity, infection and problems linked to bladder emptying.

Children with autism are just as likely to have problems with bladder control as other children. This may be more likely to occur because of reluctance to drink, reduced body awareness or trying to postpone going to the toilet.

The Paediatric Continence Forum have published a *Commissioning Guide* (2014), which now has NICE accreditation. They recommend:

> All children and young people from birth to 19 years with bladder and bowel dysfunction (continence problems), including children with learning difficulties and physical disabilities, should have access to an integrated, community-based paediatric continence service...
>
> The key Service Outcome is to help children and young people to achieve complete continence, or to manage the condition discreetly and effectively if full control is not clinically possible.

Assessment of bladder problems

This should include:

- Detailed history of urinary patterns and incontinence

- Symptoms of urinary frequency and urgency

- Bladder symptoms including pain and burning on urination

- Bowel history, especially constipation

- General health and history of any other health problems

- Developmental progress, including language and social skills

- Educational progress in school and any difficulties experienced

- Family history of bowel and bladder difficulties

- Emotional problems

- Family dynamics and stress

- Physical examination including growth, spine and abdominal examination and lower limb nerve reflexes

- Urinary specimen examination by dipstick.

Evaluation of bladder function

This should include:

- Recording of bladder frequency and patterns of wetting – bladder diaries

- Fluid intake measurement and recording

- Bowel pattern or constipation (recording diary or chart)

- Measurement of bladder volume.

Recording these details on a chart or diary can be very helpful to parents and children to help them understand the pattern of the child's problem and take part in problem solving. It can help children to become more involved and interested in the process, and the 'be a scientist' approach may be useful. Sample charts are included in the Practical Tools section.

Further investigations

The following may be considered if needed:

- Ultrasound examination of the urinary tract to identify any abnormality. This will also indicate the presence of residual urine in the bladder after urination.

- Intravenous pyelogram – an X-ray procedure to investigate the structure of the kidneys and urinary tract. This can identify conditions leading to infections such as reflux of the urine from the bladder towards the kidney.

- Urodynamic investigation looking at the bladder filling and emptying, and the pressure of bladder fluid. This helps in understanding bladder functioning.

Management of bladder problems

Management of problems will include:

- Full assessment and investigations as indicated

- Explanation advice and information to children and their families

- Adequate watery fluids (seven drinks a day), toileting programmes and reminders

- Rewards (small but interesting) for achievable targets

- Regular support and review

- Advice to school about the condition and appropriate strategies

- Information about continence protection and/or discreet pads if appropriate

- Medication if it would be helpful combined with the above

- Information about support, for example ERIC[8] (Education and Resources for Improving Childhood Continence) or PromoCon.[9]

Bladder problems causing wetting in school

It is essential that teachers and other school staff have information and advice about any bladder and bowel difficulties that may occur in school. This may include access to toilets, ensuring that everyone understands that children with bladder problems may need immediate access to the toilet without having to wait for permission to go. This is especially important as children become older and move to higher classes. It will be necessary to ensure that staff understand the child's bladder difficulties and do not think the child is getting out of lessons, or being naughty. A health or toilet pass may be useful in some schools. It is important to bear in mind that anxiety about getting to the toilet, or not being allowed to go, is likely to increase bladder problems, especially feelings of urgency.

Good liaison is essential in ensuring consistency of management of bladder problems at school and at home. It may be useful to consider some written guidelines to provide information to school staff about the child's condition, and provide suggestions for management. This would include information about toileting needs, access to the toilet, reminders, rewards and medication. Other issues such as hygiene and needs for cleaning, changing and disposal of any continence products may need to be included.

A formal health care plan may be agreed as part of a special educational needs provision. Many children with bladder problems may not be formally identified as having significant special educational needs; nevertheless, bladder difficulties do often impact on a child's educational progress, by the amount of time taken to manage these problems and also the effect on confidence and inclusion.

Good practice would always require the involvement of parents or carers. Child minders and youth group leaders may need to be

---

8   www.eric.org.uk
9   www.disabledliving.co.uk/Promocon

included in the programme if appropriate. It is usually helpful to inform any other professionals involved with the family.

All advice needs to be regularly reviewed, monitored and updated, and an agreed time to review progress of the plan should always be an agenda item (an out-of-date plan is useless and could easily be confusing to the child and professionals and hamper progress). Management strategies can be improved by considering observations and feedback from school staff and others involved with the child.

There are a number of guidelines about inclusion of children with individual needs, such as *Including Me – Managing Complex Health Needs in Schools and Early Years Settings* (Carlin 2005), which are a useful resource for ensuring provision of appropriate support. A number of local authorities have recommended guidelines for management of continence needs in school.

ERIC launched the 'Right to Go' campaign in early 2014 to highlight every child's right to good care for a continence problem at school and right to access safe and hygienic toilet facilities. Their campaign objectives include ensuring that all education settings have policies and procedures in place for continence and that school toilets are safe, hygienic and well maintained.

Some problems affecting daytime bladder control

Daytime bladder control difficulties may include the following (Nevéus *et al.* 2006):

- Bladder immaturity and small bladder capacity

- Overactive bladder and urge incontinence

- Urinary infections

- Dysfunctional voiding

- Stress incontinence

- Voiding postponement

- Vaginal reflux

- Giggle incontinence.

Note: A child who has continuous wetting and dribbling urine should have an immediate medical assessment.

Bladder immaturity and small bladder capacity

This is fairly common in young children and there is variability in the rate at which the bladder matures. The urinary system is normal and there are no structural or functional problems in bladder emptying, and it usually improves as children grow older.

In this condition, the child has a smaller than normal bladder capacity and more frequent bladder emptying. They need to have more visits to the toilet to empty the bladder and achieve dryness. They usually have less warning that they need to wee. For many children and parents this may be annoying.

An explanation of the condition is important to help everyone understand that the child is not being lazy or naughty. Regular professional support may be very helpful. Explanation to the child about how the bladder works may be useful (ERIC have a great 'kids area' on their website!). Small fun rewards given for effort, rather than success, may be a good approach. It can be helpful to focus on specific parts of the day to build up success. Many children find it easier to develop control when the day is more structured, and they are less tired. It is also important to ensure that the child has a good fluid intake (seven cups of watery drinks a day) to ensure that the urine is dilute; this also helps to develop and increase the bladder capacity.

Measurement of the bladder capacity can be helpful to understanding the difficulty and monitoring progress. The bladder capacity gradually improves as children grow older, and they also develop the capacity to anticipate and plan bladder emptying.

Overactive bladder and urge incontinence

This is a fairly common condition in which the bladder empties suddenly without warning, often when it is only partially filled. It is caused by the bladder muscle called the detrusor contracting to empty the bladder prematurely. As there is bladder contraction before complete filling, the child does not have the warning sensation of a full bladder, so is only aware of wetting at the last minute, often when it is too late.

These children find that they are suddenly wet, and have little warning when they need to wee. There is often a dash to get to the toilet, and there may be wetting accidents on the way, or in the toilet, as they can't pull their clothes down in time. They often wriggle and get into positions that help to hold the wee in. Girls may crouch onto their heel and boys hold the end of their penis. They usually can't walk to the toilet as the muscles they need for walking there are used to hold onto their wee.

It is important that the child, their family and school staff understand the condition, and know that the child is not being naughty or lazy. They are often trying hard to stay dry and may become disheartened. It can be associated with teasing or bullying, and anxiety may aggravate the condition.

Urgency and wetting may be worse if the urine becomes concentrated, and some children drink less with the idea this may help them stay drier. Some drinks aggravate the wetting, such as caffeine, quinine and artificial colourings, sweeteners and some flavourings. The effect of these drinks can vary and be individual. Constipation will make the wetting worse and a full bowel may make the bladder more irritable.

There are a range of approaches to help with bladder urgency and daytime wetting:

- Maintain a good fluid intake of watery drinks.

- Explain to children and families that the bladder empties, often before the child has the sensation they need to go.

- Arrange a programme of regular bladder emptying, with reminders linked to the daytime routine if needed. The timing for this will need to be informed by the child's pattern and bladder capacity. Visual or sign prompts may be needed. A vibrating alarm watch can be a useful reminder.

- A 'pass' to go to the toilet in school may be helpful. There are also cards from the Bowel and Bladder Foundation[10] that can be used for access to public toilets.

- Medication can be very helpful, especially as children grow older. This works by reducing the bladder muscle contractions and increasing the bladder capacity, to enable more effective bladder filling. The medication needs to be monitored with medical supervision, and the dose sometimes needs to be adjusted for individual children to obtain the best effect. There are a number of side-effects which sometimes occur, but usually these disappear if the medication is discontinued. A slow-release preparation is also available which can be useful, especially for some older children.

- If the problem persists as children grow older, it may be helpful to measure bladder activity with urodynamic investigations to clarify how the bladder is working.

Urinary infections

These can occur in children and may cause the child to be unwell with a high temperature and vomiting. There may be lower abdominal discomfort and burning on urination, and sometimes blood in the urine. The urine may be offensive and smelly, and sometimes cloudy. There is often a history of normal bladder function before the onset of the infection. There may be associated continence difficulties.

The NICE guidelines on urinary tract infection recommend urgent assessment in young children, and treatment with antibiotics if a urinary infection is thought to be present. A specimen of urine should be sent to the laboratory to identify the bacteria causing the infection and the sensitivity to antibiotics, and a renal scan should be done if there are recurrent infections.

Recurrent infections are sometimes treated with longer courses of smaller doses of antibiotics to prevent these recurring. Failure of the bladder to empty fully, leaving a presence of residual urine, can predispose to recurrent infections. Constipation can also trigger

10   www.bowelandbladderfoundation.org

urinary infections, usually by interfering with complete bladder emptying. Effective treatment of constipation and a good fluid intake can help to prevent urinary infections recurring.

Sometimes after an infection has been effectively treated, the bladder may continue to show irritability. The approaches for irritable bladder are then appropriate.

Dysfunctional voiding

This describes a condition that occurs on bladder emptying where the urethral sphincter contracts as the bladder muscle also contracts to empty. This prevents the bladder emptying effectively and causes increased pressure in the bladder. It is usually identified by urodynamic investigations. These children often need specialised input from a urology department, including biofeedback techniques and further treatment at times.

Stress incontinence

This is when wetting occurs with increased abdominal pressure, such as during coughing and sneezing. The wetting does not occur at other times. It is fairly uncommon in children, and usually occurs in women after having children. It sometimes occurs in teenagers and may be helped by specific pelvic floor exercises. These can be assisted by specialist help from a physiotherapist (many people, especially children, find it difficult to visualise and exercise the pelvic floor).

Voiding postponement

This is often seen in children who sometimes can hold on to their urine for long periods, and may manage to retain large volumes of urine. It can cause the bladder to become over-full and the children may only use the toilet very infrequently. It is usually linked to anxiety about using the toilet and resolves as they become less anxious. It is helpful to ensure a good fluid intake and calmly continue with a regular toileting routine with reminders and rewards for going to the toilet. Sitting with a fiddle toy, puzzle or game can be helpful, allowing adequate time on the toilet to enable the child to become relaxed. Blowing activities, tickling and laughing can relax the urinary sphincter. The sound of running tap water may be a helpful stimulant to urination. Analysis of any sensory differences may be appropriate.

While it can be worrying when children do empty their bladder infrequently, there is usually no damage that occurs from this.

Vaginal reflux

This occasionally happens in girls who wet within ten minutes of emptying their bladder normally. It is caused by some urine being held in the vagina, which leaks out when they stand up. It is not associated with any abnormality. It can be helped by staying on the toilet a little longer after urination to allow emptying, and sometimes by standing up and then sitting down again.

Giggle incontinence

This is a mystery. It occurs in some children, mainly girls, where the bladder completely empties on laughing. Bladder and urinary function is normal at other times, and investigations do not show any abnormality. It usually improves with age and often does not respond to intervention with training and drugs. It can be very annoying and worrying for children. It can help to give information, support, advice about protective clothing and contact with support organisations. Advice and monitoring about bullying may be needed. It is helpful to be able to tell the child that they have a genuine condition, and it is not their fault.

Chapter 10

BEDWETTING (NOCTURNAL ENURESIS)

For children, bedwetting is often upsetting, as it affects their happiness, self-confidence and friendships. There are few other medical conditions that make it so hard for children to go on sleepovers, residential school trips and camping with their friends.

It also has a large impact on families, especially on the person doing the washing and changing the bedding. Bed protection, changes in clothes and expenses linked to the extra laundry are often significant, and impact greatly upon families, especially those with limited incomes. It is very stressful for everyone, including siblings, who may not like to ask friends home to play or stay if there are signs and smells of wee in the house.

As bedwetting improves when children get older, some medical professionals perhaps don't take it as seriously as they could do. The NICE guidelines on bedwetting, published in 2010, give doctors and other professionals information and advice about the management and treatment of these children. It should be borne in mind that although bedwetting improves with age, there are a small proportion of children where it persists into adulthood.

For children with autism, delay in becoming dry at night can be especially important because of the potential impact upon their ability to develop friendships and social opportunities. These may be the experiences that are particularly important to encourage for these children. This is a problem that can be improved, helped and treated, which may help to improve the child's confidence and reduce anxiety.

How do children get dry?

We really don't know exactly, but as the bladder matures and can hold more urine, it develops the ability to hold on through the night. This is combined with children's awareness of their bladder function during toilet training and learning to be dry and to hold on until they get to the toilet. Often when children become dry during the day, they start to get dry nappies at night. It is usually suggested that after six months of being dry in the day, children are likely to be ready to become dry at night.

Interestingly, we find that most children get dry at night by learning to hold on to their wee until morning and most of them do not need to wake to go to the toilet in the night. This process is seen in all children, irrespective of their level of ability.

Advice suggested in the NICE guidelines on bedwetting includes the following:

- Inform children, young people and families that bedwetting is not the young person's fault, and punitive measures should not be used.

- Offer information, support, assessment, treatment and referral if needed.

- Consider the needs and circumstances of the child and family.

- Do not exclude younger children from intervention, but discuss their individual needs.

- Give advice on ensuring an adequate fluid intake and toileting.

Bedwetting and children with autism

Many children with autism get dry at night at the usual time. If children are reliably dry in the day for at least six months it is good to begin to consider whether it is appropriate to start night-time training, providing this will not be stressful.

The other difficulties children with autism have in socialising, education and anxiety may aggravate bedwetting, and also make it appropriate to leave intervention until some of these difficulties improve. The effort of coping with daytime demands may lead to excessive tiredness.

Many children with autism have sleep problems and any approaches to help with bedwetting should not aggravate this.

Bedwetting incidence and patterns

Primary nocturnal enuresis (bedwetting) is defined as 'involuntary wetting during sleep'. It affects about 10 per cent of seven-year-olds (which is about 3 children in every class of 30). It may help to tell children that there are likely to be another two in the class who are also not yet dry at night (Butler and Heron 2008).

There is an increased incidence of a family history of bedwetting, and boys are affected more than girls. There is a natural improvement with age, but it is important to remember that there are a small number of cases where this persists into adulthood. This has been reported as affecting up to 2–3 per cent of adults (Yeung et al. 2004).

As the condition runs in families, parents of children who wet the bed may remember their own past experiences, and this may affect their response to their children's bedwetting. Occasionally, parents may still have this problem themselves.

MYTH

Picking dandelions can make you wet the bed.

Causes of bedwetting

- Maturity of bladder control – this is a developmental skill associated with learning night-time bladder control.

- Many children have been found to have difficulty in arousing from sleep and responding to a full bladder (Nevéus *et al.* 1999). A lot of children sleep deeply, but they don't all wet the bed. There is a great deal of interest and investigation being done in how the quality of sleep and arousal operates in bedwetting.

- Some children continue to produce large amounts of urine at night. This is linked to insufficient production of a hormone called vasopressin. This is produced in the brain by the pituitary gland. Usually this hormone reduces the amount of urine produced during sleep. If there is not enough of this, the body continues to make a lot of urine during the night, making it more likely the bed will be wet. This can cause large wetting accidents, often early in the night (Rittig *et al.* 2008).

- Some children with bedwetting may have an overactive bladder, which may be associated with daytime urgency and sometimes wetting.

- There may also be a combination of some or all of these factors.

Assessment

This should include details of bedwetting and also the daytime bladder pattern. Fluid intake, bowel pattern and general health should also be explored (Vande Walle *et al.* 2012). The impact of the bedwetting on the child and family should be discussed, and the wishes and needs of the family for intervention and treatment should be taken into account.

Although the main stress of bedwetting is caused by having wet beds, additional stresses such as starting school or bullying can exacerbate the problem. The contribution of stress and anxiety is especially important to explore in children with autism.

Delay in becoming dry at night is a developmental skill which may be associated with other developmental problems. Difficulties with coordination, attention, learning or social skills may be linked with bedwetting and these should be evaluated (Vande Walle *et al.* 2012).

Fluids

Families sometimes restrict fluids, especially in the evening, but there is little evidence that this helps children to become dry at night. It is logical to discourage large amounts of fluids at bedtime and avoid drinks containing caffeine (which is a bladder stimulant) such as tea, coffee and chocolate drinks. It is also best to exclude fizzy and sugary drinks. Many children do not have a good daytime fluid intake, often because they are busy, and have immature thirst mechanisms (Kenney and Chiu 2001). It is helpful to encourage a good daytime fluid intake. Children who drink well during the day need fewer evening drinks.

Lifting

Many parents try lifting their children and taking them to the toilet after they have gone to sleep. There is no evidence that this helps children to become dry, as they may get used to passing urine in the night. If lifting increases the number of dry nights, it can help their confidence, but should only be used as a short-term strategy (NICE 2012). Rousing children in the night may affect daytime alertness and school progress, and may be stressful. The pros and cons of lifting should be discussed with parents, and it should be discontinued if it is not improving the bedwetting.

Waking up children with autism at night is usually a bad idea, as they may become upset and often have difficulty in getting back to sleep.

Night-time nappies or pull-ups

The NICE guidelines suggest that if a child has been toilet trained by day for six months, a trial without night-time nappies should be considered. There is no doubt that using nappies relieves stress on families and reduces the amount of washing. Some children manage dry nappies in the morning as their bladder becomes more mature, and this tells their families that they can be dry at night.

The use of night-time protection may reduce the motivation to get dry. Using a nappy at the same time as encouraging night-time dryness may give a mixed message to the child. Some children like to try without night-time nappies, and this can motivate them and make them feel more grown up, and sometimes this can initiate dry nights. This should be done at a good time for the family, when things are relaxed – not when there are visitors, or when starting a new class at school. It is important that discontinuing nappies does not cause more stress for families. For children with autism who find daytime social demands difficult, coming out of nappies may not be a priority.

Bed protection

Good bed protection is extremely important and reduces the stress of wet beds. There are waterproof mattresses, quilt covers, pillow cases, and absorbent bed pads (washable and disposable) and these are often very helpful. They can be purchased from many household stores, online and from ERIC. In some areas, continence nurses may be able to supply bed protection for children with disabilities.

Rewards

Many children like to have rewards, but these should be for negotiated positive behaviour, and achievable targets. This may include emptying their bladder before going to bed, helping to change the sheets, or drinking regularly during the day. For some children, praise and rewards for dry nights can create disappointment and a sense of failure if they are wet. If children are getting dry nights, they may enjoy putting rings round the date on the calendar or sometimes trying to beat their record of the number of dry nights.

Referral and treatment

Many areas provide resources and clinics to help children and families with bedwetting problems. Help may also be available from continence nurses and school nurses. Information about clinics and treatment is available from ERIC and PromoCon.

The NICE guidelines suggest that further help should be offered for the following:

- Families wishing to have further treatment and advice

- Children who are not developing night-time continence as they grow older

- Children who are concerned about the difficulty in staying away from home, school trips and participating in activities with their friends

- Children who have bedwetting with daytime wetting accidents and bladder urgency.

Do not exclude younger children, under seven years old, on the basis of age alone.

Treatment options

Training programmes

Encourage daytime fluids, bladder emptying at bed-time (and sometimes again after a story), positive thinking and rewards.

Bedwetting alarms

These are sometimes loaned from clinics, or can be purchased by families. They have a sensor that recognises when the child wets, causing the alarm to respond. Alarms have a good success rate, and help children get dry by using a conditioned reflex that links wetting with the alarm, so they learn to hold onto their wee all night until morning. They work well if children and families want to use them and the NICE guidelines recommend this as the first treatment option. They can sometimes take some time to work, so treatment needs to be persisted with. They can be demanding to use and sometimes annoying and disruptive. It is a challenge to change sheets in the middle of the night, and often children sleep through the alarm but it wakes everyone else in the house (and sometimes the neighbours too!). For children who are upset by the sound of an alarm, vibrating alarms or extension alarms to wake adults may be useful.

These alarms can work equally well for children with autism, but account will need to be taken to ensure that they do not cause anxiety or problems in getting back to sleep. Some children with autism may choose to use an alarm just in the holidays.

Medication

Desmopressin can be prescribed, and is available as melts which dissolve under the tongue, or as tablets. The medication causes the body to follow the normal diurnal pattern of urine production, reducing the amount of wee made in the night. It can be helpful to reduce bedwetting, and is well tolerated. It may be especially useful for school trips, sleepovers and holidays. It can be used for longer periods, especially in older children, and it builds their confidence and reduces the stress of wet beds.

Medication with desmopressin may be effective for children with autism, and they may sometimes have a strong preference for which product they prefer. Alarms may be combined with desmopressin, and then the medication gradually withdrawn.

Other medication

This includes anticholinergic preparations which help to reduce bladder urgency, and can help some children have dry nights. A combination of this medication and an alarm may also be used.

Tricyclic antidepressants such as imipramine are less commonly used as there is a higher incidence of side-effects, but they can work for some children.

Teenagers

Teenagers with bedwetting may not mention that this is happening. It may impact greatly on their self-esteem and participation in activities, as well as plans for further education and relationships. They need support and advice about fluids, including alcohol (beer drinking in the evening can be disastrous for these youngsters!), and about treatment options and referral. ERIC has a section for teenagers on their website.

Children who continue to wet the bed are usually very concerned about the possibility that they may never become dry, and this stress is likely to aggravate the bedwetting.

Holidays, family visits, school trips, foreign travel

Children usually want to participate in these activities and this can be a motivator for some to address their bedwetting with determination and persist with treatment. Children who continue to have wet beds need a sensitive plan to manage their bedwetting without embarrassment, to enable them to participate in activities. This may include night-time protection and arrangements to deal with wet bedding and clothes discreetly, as well as help from a sympathetic adult if needed. Sometimes when children are on trips, the excitement together with later nights may help them to be dry. Medication with desmopressin melts or tablets can be a useful option and can be taken just while they are away if needed. ERIC's downloadable leaflet 'Nights Away' is very helpful.

Alternative therapies

A number of alternative therapies are sometimes used for bed-wetting. These include acupuncture, hypnotherapy, psychotherapy, chiropractic care and medicinal herbs. The evidence for the benefit of these was evaluated in a Cochrane review (Huang *et al.* 2011), and this suggested that these may help some children, but the research information was small. They were not found to be as effective as alarms or conventional medication. They may be an option that some families may like to consider.

Information and advice for families bedwetting recommended by the NICE guidelines

- Give information about the condition
- Encourage good fluid intake – 7 drinks of clear fluid a day
- Bladder emptying at bedtime
- Information about bed protection and night-time nappies
- Discuss pros and cons of lifting to toilet during the night
- Give contact details about support and information
- Interesting, but not too big, rewards for achievable targets
- Positive thinking
- Arrange further referral if needed – younger children should not be excluded.

Chapter 11

THE BOWEL AND HOW IT WORKS

Many children with autism have problems at some time with bowel activity, and so do children who do not have autism. Sometimes this is not discussed with other parents or professionals, but these problems can be treated and improved and usually resolved.

Many of the difficulties with bowel control in children with autism are linked to not understanding what they should do, and stress associated with coping with change. Bowel patterns in children are often unpredictable, which may be difficult for children with autism to understand and respond to. In addition, their bowel pattern is often affected by restricted eating and drinking patterns, constipation, and sometimes food sensitivity. Anxiety about toilets and letting the poo go may lead to holding in their poo, something many children are very good at, and this will cause an irregular bowel pattern and is often linked to constipation.

Poo!!

Many people do not like poo. The smell, the inconvenience, and for most children it can be uncomfortable to pass at times, as well as being boring to sit on the toilet to wait until it comes out. Learning to use the toilet to open the bowels for many children and parents is difficult and stressful. Children often learn that it is much easier to do their poo in a comfortable nappy, or hold it in and carry on playing. Many children get very good at holding their poo in by contracting their anal muscles. They can sometimes get into funny positions to hold onto their poo, and may cross their legs and stretch backwards and tighten their muscles – the 'banana position'.

Normal poo is soft and is usually able to pass through the anus without discomfort; the anus is designed so that it can stretch. The normal bowel contracts to move the poo along and can contain wind too. Occasionally these normal bowel contractions may be uncomfortable. Children may learn that this is to be avoided at all costs.

At times children may be off colour with a cold or childhood illness, and eat differently or not drink enough. This may make the poo harder so it is uncomfortable to pass, and the child may learn to try to stop this happening again. Any discomfort on opening the bowels may lead to a continued pattern of avoiding pooing by withholding, leading to constipation. Lots of things can change the bowel pattern: different food, eating routines, travel, illness, different drinks and anxiety. The rigid diets that often occur in children with autism can increase the likelihood of constipation. The irritability and lack of appetite, linked to constipation, may increase this.

How the bowel works

Food is necessary to make children grow, be healthy and have energy and fun. Eating and meal times are important social activities in every culture.

Food moves from the mouth and gullet to the stomach, where it is mixed with enzymes that digest it. It then passes through the small bowel where digestion continues and the nutrients the body needs are absorbed. The products remaining after the digestion enter the large bowel starting in the right lower abdomen. A wave-like activity of the muscles in the bowel wall moves the remaining material along the large bowel. During this journey excess water is reabsorbed to conserve fluid, and the waste products finally enter the rectum. This is the storage area where faeces collect until the bowel is ready to be emptied.

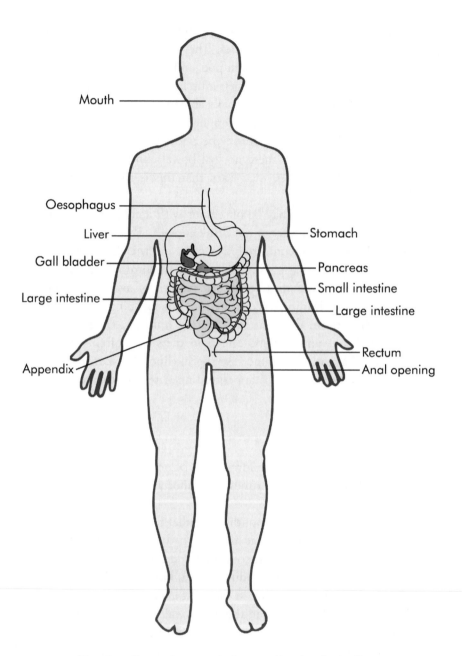

The digestive system, route from eating to elimination

As the rectum fills, this produces a sensation that is transmitted to the brain, which indicates the need to have a poo. Normally, this feeling can be suppressed until it is convenient to empty the bowel. During evacuation (having a poo), the anal sphincter relaxes to allow the bowel to empty, and the abdominal muscles contract to help increase abdominal pressure and push the poo out.

Understanding bowel patterns

Digestion and the formation of waste can have wide individual variation, and may be influenced by diet and fluid intake, as well as health problems. There is a big variation in the normal bowel pattern from two to three times a day to two to three times a week. Bowel activity can be predictable in some people, but there are often more variations in children.

Changes in diet, fluids, activity level and general health may alter the bowel pattern. It can be helpful to understand a child's individual pattern and any factors that may affect this.

THE BRISTOL STOOL FORM SCALE

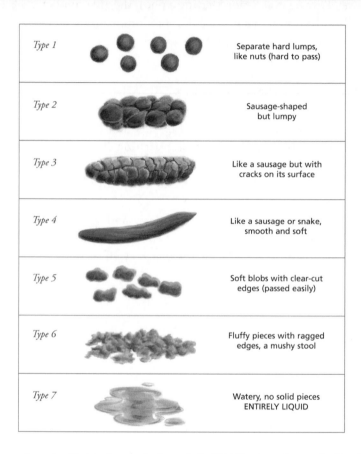

Type 1		Separate hard lumps, like nuts (hard to pass)
Type 2		Sausage-shaped but lumpy
Type 3		Like a sausage but with cracks on its surface
Type 4		Like a sausage or snake, smooth and soft
Type 5		Soft blobs with clear-cut edges (passed easily)
Type 6		Fluffy pieces with ragged edges, a mushy stool
Type 7		Watery, no solid pieces ENTIRELY LIQUID

Reproduced with kind permission of Dr KW Heaton, formerly Reader in Medicine at the University of Bristol. © 2000 produced by Norgine Pharmaceuticals Limited.

The Bristol Stool Form Scale illustrates visually the variations in types of poo and may be useful to use as a way of monitoring how the bowel is working and noticing any changes in consistency. Normal poo should look like a soft sausage – type 4 on the chart.

As well as looking at the shape and consistency of the faeces, it is also important to be aware of the size and frequency of the bowel pattern. Sometimes a child can pass small amounts of poo every day, but not fully empty their bowels, and there can be a gradual build-up of poo leading to constipation. When the bowel has fully emptied, there should be a time interval before it empties again to allow the large bowel to fill.

Where there are concerns about the bowel, it can often be useful to keep a record of the type and frequency of bowel action. This can often be done with the child to help them understand how their bowel works, together with explanations, stories and pictures. Older children may sometimes enjoy keeping a graph or visual record of their bowel pattern. It will help them to learn how their body works, and the reason for toilet training.

Factors influencing bowel function include:

- Individual variation

- Familial patterns

- Food sensitivity

- Emotional factors

- Withholding stools (voluntary or involuntary)

- Constipation.

It is important always to remember that the bowel and urinary system may influence each other.

The bowel and urinary system work together in managing the body's fluid balance. Their position is anatomically close in the lower part of the abdomen and the rectum is behind the bladder. If the bowel is full, and especially if it is constipated, it may press on the bladder and cause irritation, frequency of urination and sometimes obstruction.

Control of the bowel and bladder

Most of the control of internal functioning is by the autonomic nervous system, which when it is functioning normally is not perceived consciously, so we are not aware of its activity.

Part of the autonomic system is the sympathetic nervous system, which operates as part of the 'flight or fight' mechanism, and is influenced by adrenaline hormones. As part of the 'preparation for action' fight or flight response, this will normally prevent or postpone bowel and bladder emptying. This helps to explain some of the effects of stress on bowel patterns, and it is hard for a child to empty the bowel when they are anxious.

Gastrocolic reflex

This is a useful thing to know about, and describes the action of the bowel in normal digestion. After eating, the whole bowel becomes more active. As the food is digested, other products in the digestive tract move along as the bowel contracts in a wave movement. This means that any products in the large bowel may also move towards the rectum, and in many people, especially children, there is increased likelihood of a bowel action 15 to 30 minutes after eating. This may be a good time to consider encouraging a child to try to poo. If children at school are in the playground after lunch they may need access to the toilet, or may be more likely to have soiling accidents, especially if they have to wait to access the toilet.

Problems with bowel control

Many children have problems with soiling and bowel control, and this includes some children with autism. The problems are most commonly linked to irregular bowel activity, usually caused by constipation and withholding stools. These conditions are interlinked and often aggravate each other.

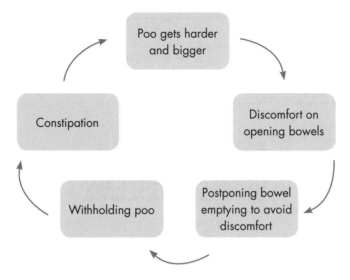

The constipation cycle

The first rule of toileting for poo problems

Our first rule is to make sure that the child and family develop a team approach to win against poo, which can be very tricky at times. The child may need a great deal of reassurance, but it is often very helpful for them to be involved as much their abilities allow. It can help to give the child the key role in the team, such as in football the child may be the goal scorer, and the parents can be the trainer and manager. Other analogies can be used if more appropriate for the family.

We often find that fathers are brilliant at thinking of innovative ways of problem solving, such as in graphs of bowel pattern or interesting rewards such as goal practice – they also may be less keen on helping with managing poo. Don't forget grandparents, and other relatives who may be able to help. They will also need to have information about the child's difficulties.

> One six-year-old boy found it great to email his granny a picture of his poo when he managed to do this (we did move on to other achievements to photograph and included pictures of clean pants).

Chapter 12

BOWEL PROBLEMS

Constipation, overflow and withholding

Constipation and withholding occur in some children with autism and this may have a devastating effect upon their health, education and interactions. It can be difficult to manage because of the complexity of factors contributing to this problem and the long time needed to resolve it. This chapter focuses more on the physical factors that are involved, but it is important to evaluate the contribution of the autism and integrate approaches to the management of the bowel difficulties.

Constipation

This is by far the most important and common cause of problems with bowel control. It occurs in many children with bowel control difficulties, including many with autism.

Constipation occurs in around 5–30 per cent of children (NICE 2010; van den Berg *et al.* 2006). The NICE guidelines on constipation make clear recommendations about the importance of identifying any underlying disease causing the problems, and referring these promptly for specialist assessment and opinion. The important alert signs include a history of constipation from birth, weakness in the lower limbs and abdominal distension with vomiting.

Most children who have constipation are healthy and do not have any underlying disease or abnormality. The cause in these children is not fully understood, though it is sometimes linked to a family history of constipation. It is essential to identify constipation in children as it needs medical treatment – failure to do this can lead to the problem continuing for a long time.

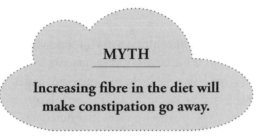

MYTH

Increasing fibre in the diet will make constipation go away.

Constipation does not get better by changing the diet alone, although this can help to prevent it and stop it recurring (NICE 2010).

When children are constipated, the large bowel becomes distended. Often, especially when this has been present for some time, there is a lack of the usual awareness of a full bowel. Children then do not experience sensation of the need to empty their bowels and often become confused about this and what adults are telling them. In addition, sensations may be felt in the abdomen while the poo comes out of their bottom: very mystifying!

The longer that poo stays inside the bowel, the larger and harder it will become and it will then hurt even more when it comes out. This can quickly become a cycle, with the child doing everything they can to avoid the pain of pooing. The memory of painful poo can stay with a child for many years, even when the problem has resolved.

Withholding

Constipation is often associated with withholding – an episode of uncomfortable constipation leading to reluctance in opening the bowels – and the withholding can then increase the constipation.

If a child has an unpleasant or painful experience in having a poo, they will naturally not want to repeat this. When they next feel the urge to have a poo, they may try to ignore the signals and keep the poo inside in order to avoid any further pain.

Withholding is linked to anxiety, which may also be about using toilets, wanting a nappy or worry about what will happen to the poo. It is, after all, something that belongs to the child from inside them that is often hard to let go.

Overflow soiling

This describes a common condition in children who are constipated. Because the rectum is full and is not emptying, soft loose poo from higher in the large bowel leaks round the constipated area and out into the pants or nappy. Because this is loose it is sometimes thought to be diarrhoea. One of the important differences from a tummy bug is that the child is well and eating, without any vomiting. The illustration shows how soft poo from higher up in the bowel may move round the larger lumps of hard poo and leak out.

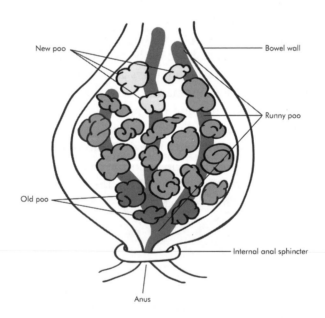

Overflow soiling

It is essential for children, parents and others caring for the child to understand that when the bowel wall is stretched, especially when this has occurred for some time, a sensation of a full bowel is not felt. The leaking occurs without any control or volition and the child usually only feels it afterwards. Telling adults often results in an expression of annoyance, and sometimes anger, so children soon stop doing this. Everyone often suppresses things they don't like and children get very good at suppressing the feel and smell of poo, even when everyone else notices.

Factors that may affect constipation

- Diet without enough fibre (but remember a high fibre diet won't help bowel regularity without an adequate fluid intake)

- Inadequate fluids

- Holding onto the poo

- Anxieties about monsters, snakes or crocodiles in the toilet

- Being unwell, colds, high temperature

- Sometimes it just happens.

In addition, children with autism may also have:

- Sensory differences that can mean they find toilets uncomfortable and frightening

- Limited understanding of how their body works and the sensations they are receiving

- Difficulty in appreciating that this is what they should do

- Dislike of change – such as having to poo in the toilet

- Learnt that a nappy is where the poo goes

- Anxiety in new situations, such as school

- Anxieties about the splash from the toilet water

- Problems in using different toilets.

It can be difficult to know when children are constipated, and it may be useful to watch the type and frequency of their bowel pattern, and keep a record of this to discuss with a health professional.

Signs of constipation

- Fewer than three complete stools a week
- 'Rabbit droppings' (type 1 on the Bristol Stool Form Scale)
- Huge poos that only occasionally happen and can block the toilet
- Poor appetite and irritability that gets better after a poo
- Abdominal pain and/or discomfort, especially if there has not been a proper poo recently
- Observed retentive posturing, with straight legs, tiptoes and arched back – the 'banana position'
- Straining when trying to poo
- Anal pain and sometimes bleeding when the poo is passed.

It is always advisable to have a medical assessment including a physical examination, with a growth and abdominal examination. It may be possible to feel the large bowel swollen and full of hard faeces. If the child is healthy it is not usually necessary to do any further investigations.

There are a few things that may suggest an abnormality, when further investigation should be arranged (NICE 2010):

- Constipation originating from birth or the first few weeks of life
- Failure to pass meconium (the sticky greenish substance a baby passes in the first few days after birth)
- 'Ribbon stools' (thin stools that could suggest narrowing of the large bowel)

- Abdominal swelling and vomiting which could mean there is a blockage of the bowel.

The treatment of constipation

This needs to be done in two stages (NICE 2010):

1. *Disimpaction* using laxatives in sufficient doses to clear the bowel. If not enough laxative is given, it may just make more runny poo come out without moving the large lump of poo blocking the rectum.

2. *Maintenance* doses of laxatives. These may need to be given for a long time, often for several years. The dose may need to be adjusted and parents should be advised by the health professional treating the child how to do this to ensure there is a regular bowel pattern.

A guide for the length of treatment often given is: at least for as long as the constipation has been present. It is safe to use medication for long periods, though like any medication it should be monitored by a medical professional.

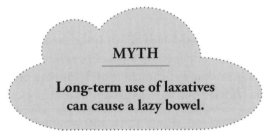

MYTH

Long-term use of laxatives can cause a lazy bowel.

The medication does not cause the development of a lazy bowel. If the large bowel is continually stretched by constipation it will not work so well. Recurrent and persistent constipation is therefore much more dangerous and debilitating for a child than any risks linked with long-term medication.

Note: Often the amount of medication needed can be above the licensed dose for children, or sometimes unlicensed medication may be needed. It is recognised in the British National Formulary that this may be required at times.

In addition, the following are needed:

- Regular support for children and families and monitoring of the effectiveness of medication.

- Very careful discontinuation of medication, which should only be done when there has been a regular bowel pattern for some time; reducing the medication too soon may cause the constipation to recur.

- Continued monitoring of the bowel pattern, and restart of treatment immediately if the constipation recurs.

- Healthy eating, with plenty of fibre and clear fluids (if possible). Young children, who still drink a lot of milk, may not be getting hungry and eating enough fibre. Milk may reduce their thirst so they will not have enough clear fluids.

- Intervention and information to help with children's anxiety about toileting and to build their confidence. The fear of a painful poo often lasts a long time long after the constipation is treated and may take a long time to resolve.

- Trying to make toileting fun with rewards for achievable targets, games and apps.

- It is essential for the muscles to be relaxed to allow the poo out, and this is helped by a good position with a footstool, a toilet seat that fits the child and support on the sides if needed. Advice may be needed about correct positioning.

- Many people feel that a squatting position helps effective bowel function, and for some children and young people a 'Squatty Potty' may help (see Resources). In many parts of the world a squatting position is usual and encouraged by the design of toilets.

- Stories about poo and how the body works, such as *Poo Go Home* (Black n.d.).

- Social Stories™ specific for the child.

- Bubbles, blowing toys or tickling to promote relaxation; these activities make it more difficult to hold the poo inside.

- Exercise – it is difficult to hold the poo in when you are jumping or bouncing, or during activities such as horse riding. Exercise is also good for relaxation and wellbeing.

Management of constipation, withholding and soiling/pooing accidents is complex and needs a long-term approach. It is essential that time is spent explaining the condition and the mechanism to families and children.

Treatment is often needed for a long time to re-establish a regular bowel pattern and to maintain this. It is common for this treatment to be required for a number of years. Ensuring that families fully understand the condition ensures that they are able to be active partners in management of their child's condition, with understanding and commitment in persisting with long-term treatment and management. There are some good resources for parents in the Bibliography; particularly useful is the guide by Anthony Cohn, *Constipation, Withholding and Your Child.*

When a normal regular bowel pattern has become re-established, medication can be withdrawn; this usually needs to be done gradually and carefully to prevent any recurrence of the constipation. This can be done by reducing the dose or giving the same dose less frequently. Regular monitoring of the bowel pattern is essential and treatment will need to be restarted if the constipation recurs.

Medication for constipation

Some rules for giving oral treatment:

- Find out what the child (and parents) can take, considering taste, amount and acceptability. Medication that is prescribed that the child thinks is disgusting to taste is not likely to be taken reliably, and is quite likely to be spat out, hidden or poured away secretly!

- Recognise that trying to get children to swallow medicine they dislike can be extremely stressful for parents.

- Make sure that medication is given in doses that are enough to work effectively. If the medication does not effectively empty the bowels, the runny poo from above can leak out and cause accidents, meaning the blockage is still there. There is nothing worse and more likely to cause parents to stop treatment than continuing to have soiled, smelly underwear.

- While there are recommendations for dosage, the amount needed to work effectively for children can be very individual.

- The frequency of medication may need to be adjusted as well as the dose. We have sometimes found that a larger dose of medication given every second or third day can work effectively for some children.

- Give regular support, and monitor the medication regularly.

- Make sure that grandparents are on board if they are involved.

Types of medication

Oral medication consists of treatments to soften the stool, make it more bulky or stimulate the muscles in the bowel wall to push to poo out. It can be useful to combine a stool softener with a small amount of stimulant as well.

With all oral medications it can be difficult to predict how long they will take to work, and there needs to be a bit of trial and error to get the dose right. This may cause difficulties in school, so there is a need for detailed explanations and ongoing communication with staff.

Some treatments for constipation

	Advantages	Disadvantages
Macrogols Polyethylene Glycol e.g. Movicol	Recommended in the NICE guidelines as the first treatment for constipation; disimpaction treatment followed by a regular maintenance dose. This is an effective, safe medication and easy to take. It comes as a powder that needs to be mixed with water. It can be concealed in squash, milk, and soup or other favourite foods if needed. The child needs to have fluids for it to work effectively. There is also a chocolate flavoured liquid available. The dose needs regular monitoring and adjusting for a smooth effect.	Some children don't like the taste. It can be difficult to drink the amount of water and liquids needed. The effect can be unpredictable in some children. They can have loose stools, especially if the bowel is not effectively disimpacted.
Lactulose	This is a liquid and works by drawing fluid into the bowels so makes the stool bulky, soft and slippery. It is a safe, mild laxative, and tastes sweet so children usually like it.	It is sometimes not strong enough to be effective. It is not good for dental health, especially as medication is often needed for long periods. Occasionally some children may be lactose intolerant.

	Advantages	Disadvantages
Senna	This is derived from a natural plant extract, and works by stimulating the bowel muscles, so the poo is pushed along more quickly and less fluid is reabsorbed by the bowel. It can be given as a liquid, tablets or granules (which can be sprinkled on cereals and other food).	It can sometimes cause tummy cramps. Children may find the taste disgusting.
Sodium Docusate	This works as both a stimulant and bulking agent. It comes as a liquid and capsules.	Capsules can be difficult to swallow. The liquid may not taste nice to a child.
Sodium Picosulphate	This is a strong stimulant and may be useful if other medications haven't worked. It is less likely to be used as a regular medication. It comes as liquid and small capsules (perles).	It may be too strong and cause a poo explosion! It may cause diarrhoea and tummy cramps.
Bisacodyl	It comes as liquid, tablets and suppositories. It is a bowel stimulant and is another option.	It may cause tummy ache or sickness.
Syrup of figs	This is available over the counter from chemists. It can work for some constipation and some children may like the taste. If it works, hooray!	It may not be strong enough. It is not on prescription, so families have to buy it.

Suppositories	These are inserted into the anus. These are not often used in children. They can give a quick and more predictable effect. *One of the teenagers treated preferred this so she could go to her part-time job without any uncertainty! She also hated taking oral medication.* In some cultures this is a standard way of giving most medical treatment.	Many children will not like things put into their bottoms, and may be frightened. It may be distressing for parents to use.
Enemas	Medication is inserted into the rectum, usually in hospital. It is effective and useful for treatment of severe impaction of stools filling the bowel. It can be useful where oral medication has not worked. It can help children realise the seriousness of their bowel problem.	Children often find this frightening and upsetting. Most doctors would prefer to avoid this. It has to be followed by some maintenance therapy so the constipation does not recur.
Antegrade colonic enemas	This involves a small operation to create an opening into the bowel in the lower right abdomen. Fluid is inserted regularly and this washes the poo out of the large bowel. This is occasionally considered for the very few children where oral medication just isn't working. It may be worth it to get continent where everything else has failed, and gives the child control.	No one wants to have surgery and doctors will always avoid this unless other things have been really tried and none of these have worked.

Helping families of children with autism who have bowel difficulties

Managing constipation is nearly always very stressful. Families and children need regular support, advice and monitoring of any medication on a regular basis.

When the condition has existed for some time, families can be ruled by poo and the anxiety that accidents will occur when they are out, visiting friends and on holiday. A great deal of time and expense is spent on cleaning children and their clothes.

When a child is smelly they may not get as much time sitting with parents or being cuddled. Dealing with the problem takes so much time that this can reduce the opportunity for playing or being read to. Parents of children with autism will often have many anxieties about their child's other needs too.

We all know that poo sometimes does not smell very nice! When the bowel is constipated the poo has been inside for longer, so it is often much smellier and sometimes also sticky. This makes management of soiling accidents unpleasant and time-consuming. The child soon learns that poo is horrid and upsets people and often becomes very anxious and sad. This can affect their confidence and progress in school and may have a profound effect on building friendships. Bullying, verbal or physical, is a constant risk for children with any type of continence difficulty, but particularly if they are smelly. It can be very difficult to convince children that poo is good and needs to come out, especially when there has been a long history of soiling accidents.

It is always important to assess the emotional impact of bowel problems on both children and their families. Regular professional contact is valuable, and where necessary further help and assessment from children's mental health services, psychology, play therapy and family support services may be helpful. A joint approach in supporting the child and family will be needed.

Specialist advice for children for children with autism and eating problems may contribute to effective management. A dietician can do a nutritional assessment and give advice about eating patterns and types of food to try.

Some things that have been found useful in helping children to eat better include:

- Regular eating times, and including these on timetables
- Giving drinks after meals
- Bran flakes and raisin chocolate crispy clusters
- Lots of fibre; this can be disguised in homemade flapjacks and biscuits
- Adding fibre or lentils to pasta sauce, stews and casseroles
- Liquidising vegetables into soup
- Making pastry and biscuits with ground nuts
- Syrup tarts with high fibre cereals in the syrup, and dried fruit too if possible
- Prune puree in yogurt, ice cream or custard
- Putting pureed fruit in jelly, yogurt and in ice cream
- Small portions – praise for half a pea may be the start of progressing to five peas
- Encouraging the child to be a scientist and experiment with tastes sometimes before swallowing new foods
- Cooking with children
- Convincing children that they will be able to kick a football or run faster if they eat well!
- Lots of praise and no nagging.

Abdominal massage

There is some evidence that this can help with constipation by stimulating the action of the bowel muscles, increase the frequency of bowel movements and reduce discomfort and pain associated with constipation (Sinclair 2011; McClurg and Lowe-Strong2011).

This can be helpful for some children, especially those who enjoy tactile experiences. It can help with promoting relaxation, and also help with constipation. It is necessary to obtain guidance and instruction from a professional with experience in teaching massage for children with special needs. It is often an enjoyable experience for parents. It can be included with other approaches and treatments. A recent evaluation of massage in children with disabilities showed that there was a reduction in constipation medication needed (Bromley 2014).

Help in school

Good liaison with school staff is essential, with regular meetings and written information if appropriate. This ensures that the condition is understood by teachers and other school staff. In this way the approaches to the child's problem are consistent, and communication and language used is the same at school and at home. School staff may need support and advice to manage a child with bowel problems – this is something they have not covered in their training.

There may need to be provision for cleaning and changing in school, and this will require adequate space and facilities. There may need to be a plan detailing where to keep soiled clothes and how to hand them to the child's carers in a discreet way (not in front of other parents!).

Easy access to an 'emergency pack' for toileting and changing should be agreed. Good liaison with parents and carers to ensure that spare clothes are always available will be needed.

Young children who have soiling episodes often may need adult help in cleaning and changing. While it is constructive to encourage children to take as much responsibility as possible, this should be consistent with the child's capability and understanding. The actions needed to help change and clean soiled children should be agreed with parents. It will often be necessary to identify which school members of staff will be responsible for the child's toileting programme and help with cleaning and changing.

Reminders, signs, verbal cues or objects of reference to try to go to the toilet in time may be needed for some children. Reminders with vibrating watches can be useful for others. About twenty minutes after lunch may be a good time to try to go to the toilet, to use the gastrocolic reflex. Another time to consider is at the end of the school day. Children sometimes can hold their poo in at school, and have accidents when they get to the end of the day and are tired. This can sometimes happen when they are walking home.

It is often suggested that children should know when they are soiled and need to be changed. While this is logical it often doesn't happen. Some children may be able to use a secret code word or sign to indicate their need to be changed, and letting the child choose this gives them some control.

Requiring parents to come into school to change soiled children is a breach of equality legislation. There will, however, be some parents who do not wish others to clean their children, and some children who will only want their parents to do this.

Food sensitivities and allergies

There are many concerns about these, especially for children with autism. There is very little clear research into this area.

Food sensitivities

Food sensitivities are more likely to occur in younger children with immature bowels, and can be triggered by bowel infections. They are usually associated with irregular bowel patterns, loose smelly bowel actions and abdominal discomfort. They can be linked to the amount of trigger food eaten, and problems occurring following the intake of larger amounts of food which they are sensitive to.

These sensitivities often improve with time, and can gradually resolve. They can be linked with almost any food, but the commonest are cow's milk protein (lactose), wheat and fish. While fibre is good for bowel regularity, we have sometimes found that young children have difficulty in digesting diets with a high fibre content.

Where food sensitivity is suspected it is always useful to keep a food and symptom diary to clarify triggers for any bowel problems. After this a trial of excluding the suspect food can be done for three to four weeks, followed by a gradual re-introduction, to confirm that this is the food that is causing problems.

It is important that children with autism are not put on exclusion diets without careful evaluation, and that the effects of these are monitored. Many children with autism have very restricted eating patterns, and cutting out foods can decrease the food available for them. Often alternative foods may not be acceptable to the child – they may only like one variety or colour of a certain food. The advice of a paediatric dietician and a nutritional assessment can be very helpful and provide support and information to families.

Food allergies

True food allergies are less common than food sensitivities and often occur in children with other forms of allergy, asthma, eczema or hay fever. There is also likely to be a strong family history of allergy. Where food allergy is suspected, the child should be referred to an allergy specialist for investigations and assessment. Tests for food allergy may be useful, but sometimes the positive findings do not always link closely to the child's observed bowel pattern.

PART 4

UNDERSTANDING BEHAVIOUR

Chapter 13

SENSORY DIFFERENCES IN AUTISM

See behaviour...think sensory

> Reality to an autistic person is a confusing interacting mass
> of events, people, places, sounds and sights... A large part of
> my life is spent just trying to work out the pattern behind
> everything. *(Jolliffe, Landsdown and Robinson 1992)*

Human beings are all sensory creatures! We experience ourselves
and the world around us through our senses, but we are not aware
of the majority of this sensory input. Most people have the ability
to filter out the awareness of a great deal of the sensory information
that surrounds them. People with autism may not be able to do this
so well, therefore they can become easily overwhelmed.

We have emotional reactions to sensory experiences, which are
often influenced by memory and imagination as well as the physical
sensation. There are some sensory experiences which we may love,
such as the feel of a particular material or watching glowing embers,
whereas there may be others which we dislike, such as the sound of
fingernails on a chalkboard or a particular smell. We all appreciate
sensory experiences differently, with sometimes highly individual
emotional reactions to these.

Sensory processing

Sensory information is received from our bodies and the environment through the seven sensory systems: tactile, vestibular, proprioception, visual, auditory, olfactory and gustatory. The brain very quickly organises and interprets this information, deciding which it needs to pay attention to, what is the significance, and whether or how to respond.

Ayres (2005) describes this process as a bit like directing traffic:

> The brain locates, sorts and orders sensations, somewhat as a traffic officer directs moving cars. When sensations flow in a well-organised or integrated manner, the brain uses those sensations to form perceptions, behaviours and learning. When the flow of sensations is disorganised, life can be like a rush-hour traffic jam. (p.5)

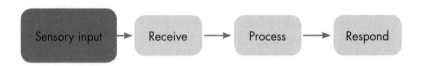

Once we receive sensory input, whether or not we become consciously aware of it, how we feel about it and how we respond to it will vary and is dependent on a range of factors, including our previous sensory experiences or how alert or stressed we are.

As we are constantly surrounded by sensory input, the brain is programmed to balance this, and we unconsciously learn to suppress awareness of much of the extra information that we process automatically, and do not need to respond to. If we were to try to pay attention to every bit of information coming in, we would be completely overwhelmed. An important part of the process is our emotional response to the input, interpreting whether it is something we enjoy or if it is something potentially harmful. This can determine how we respond; for example, if we find a smell particularly nasty, we may cover our nose and mouth to try and avoid it.

Sensory differences in children with autism

Many children with autism experience sensation differently. It is now commonly recognised that individuals with autism often have differences in sensory processing. Laurie (2013) describes how it is thought that about two-thirds of people with autism have sensory processing disorder.

The way in which a child with autism experiences the world through their senses can be very different from the way other people may experience it:

- *Hypersensitivity.* This describes how sensation is perceived more intensely. Certain noises may feel unbearably loud, smells may be perceived as completely overwhelming, and touch may feel painful. These intense experiences can cause anxiety or even physical pain. Some of these children may actively *avoid* sensory input.

- *Hyposensitivity.* This describes the awareness of sensation that is reduced and the child doesn't appear to register it. They may not be aware of strong smells or extremes of temperature, and they may not notice if they hurt themselves. In order to try and make sense of the world, some of these children actively *seek* increased sensory input. They are the children who sometimes rock, spin or slap their hands as this stimulates sensory experiences, assists with balance and posture and helps to deal with stress.

These different reactions can vary across the senses, meaning that children may crave input from one sense but actively avoid it in another. The same child may be hypersensitive to touch while being hyposensitive to smell, and this can be very difficult to understand and appreciate.

A child could have great enjoyment of spinning (vestibular hyposensitivity/ seeking behaviour), at the same time as being terrified by the fan in the bathroom (auditory hypersensitivity/avoidance behaviours)

- *Filtering difficulties.* Some children have difficulties with selecting which sensory input to pay attention to and which to ignore. If there is too much sensory information being received, a child may miss the specific input that needs attention, such as from a full bladder. Some children may be overly aware of all the noises and smells around them and then miss hearing verbal instructions that are being given from their parents or teacher.

- *Sensory defensiveness.* Some children may react negatively or with fear to sensory input that is considered inoffensive to others. They may be interpreting the information as potentially harmful, therefore experiencing high levels of anxiety with it. A child may exhibit defensive reactions to any of the senses, as a response to finding particular sensations highly distressing:

  > 'My son could not walk on carpets as the sensation on his feet was painful. We had to remove the carpet in the bathroom to allow him to go in there in bare feet.' *(Father of 14-year-old with autism)*

Sensory aspects of toileting

Toileting, like eating, is an extremely sensory experience. If a child with autism experiences differences in sensory processing, there may be several aspects of using the toilet that could cause challenges. They may find the bathroom environment distracting, upsetting or frightening or have difficulties in understanding the sensations experienced by their own body.

Yack, Sutton and Aquilla (2002) discuss the potential difficulties that some children may experience in receiving and interpreting the sensory input that signals a full bladder or the need to have a poo. They go on to explain that the bowel and bladder are smooth muscles, therefore the sensory signals they send to the brain may be like soft whispers in comparison with messages being received from other parts of the body.

Many people with autism have described feeling limited sensations from their body. This will have a profound impact on their ability to appreciate, respond and learn about bowel and bladder function. Children and young people who do not perceive and recognise the signals may need continued reminders, prompts and alarms to go to the toilet.

The seven senses...

Tactile

Touch provides information about the environment, objects and textures around us. This includes information such as whether things are hard, soft, sharp, dull, hot, cold or painful to the touch. There is a higher concentration of touch receptors on the hands and genitals.

Children who are hypersensitive or sensory avoiders (receiving too much sensory input) may struggle with sitting on toilet seats, which they experience as too hard or cold. They could be upset by wee or poo touching their hands or body, or feeling splashes of water from the toilet. They may experience discomfort or distress from the sensation of toilet roll or wipes, or solid or liquid soaps. The texture of clothing, labels, nappies or pants may feel uncomfortable. Tactile experiences from the environment, including bathroom furniture and the feel of flooring, may need to be considered.

Children who are hyposensitive or sensory seekers (not receiving much sensory input) may not notice when they are wet or soiled, and may gain tactile experience from touching or manipulating their poo. They may like the sensation of wee and poo in their pants or nappy or the input gained from wearing a nappy. They may focus on exploring the sensations received from playing with bathroom products.

Vestibular

The *balance* system provides information about our movement and where our body is in space. It gives information about our position, to know if we are upright, to understand the sensation from gravity, and cope with the information about balance derived from head position and movement.

Children who are hypersensitive or sensory avoiders may struggle with feeling balanced on the toilet, particularly if their feet can't touch the floor. The memory of previous experiences of being unstable can continue to affect children's perception. Some children find that an open space or gap at the side of the toilet affects their spatial awareness and balance and they may feel more secure in toilet cubicles with walls on either side of them. The reflections from tiling or mirrors or changes in floor surfaces may make them feel unsteady.

Children who are hyposensitive or sensory seekers may feel a need to rock to stimulate their balance system and find it difficult to sit still on the toilet.

Proprioception

This describes *body awareness*, and tells us where our body is in relation to the world around us. It helps us know which parts of our body are moving and how, and allows us to control movements without looking. It also gives information about the amount of pressure needed to manipulate objects.

Children who are hypersensitive or sensory avoiders may find it difficult to change their body position, which will affect activities such as reaching toilet paper or leaning forward when they need to wipe their bottom.

Children who are hyposensitive or sensory seekers may struggle with inadequate sensation and may enjoy the deep pressure they get from wearing a nappy. Nappies and tight clothing may stimulate their body to be more aware and help with experiencing and coordinating their body movements. They may not know how to correctly position themselves on the toilet or where to place their feet. Some children may try to sense where they are by pushing themselves back against the toilet cistern. They may appear to be clumsy and bump into the sink or trip over clothes left on the bathroom floor.

The toilet roll may be found in different positions in bathrooms, causing both confusion to locate it and difficulties with reaching it. Children often find wiping themselves difficult. This could be due to problems in coordinating their movements or finding the right amount of pressure to clean themselves effectively.

Visual

Sight provides information about objects and people around us, enabling us to define the boundaries of things we can see.

Children who are hypersensitive or sensory avoiders may struggle with the confusing amount of visual stimulation in a bathroom. This can come from bright lights or reflections from tiling, mirrors or windows. They may be overwhelmed by the range of colourful toiletry products, towels or patterned flooring. This visual input may cause distraction and sometimes anxiety and distress.

Children who are hyposensitive or sensory seekers may focus on the light reflection instead of what they are supposed to be doing in the bathroom.

Auditory

Hearing provides information about the sounds around us – whether they are loud, soft, high, low, near or far.

Children who are hypersensitive or sensory avoiders may struggle with the variety and volume of sounds within a bathroom – echoes, water running, flushing toilets, fans, and so on. Some children may find the sound of wee or poo landing in the toilet worrying. Hand-dryers can be particularly difficult for some, and have been described as making a loud and painful sound. In school or public toilets, other people may cause additional noises and confusion.

Children who are hyposensitive or sensory seekers may be unaware of or actively seek out some of the sounds within the bathroom. They may enjoy the sound of the toilet flush, and they may want to play with this rather than using the toilet. Some may enjoy the echoes in a bathroom.

Olfactory

This provides information about different types and varieties of *smell*, many of which are present in different bathroom products. The experience of smell is a very emotional experience and highly individual. It is often closely linked to unconscious previous experiences. The smells some people like can be very distressing for others.

Children who are hypersensitive or sensory avoiders may find certain smells unpleasant or distressing. These smells could include wee and poo: their own or other people's. Manufacturers often insert strong perfumes in toiletries and cleaning products which can be overwhelming, especially in a small bathroom or following frequent use. Smelly items such as dirty laundry or clean towels are often stored in the bathroom, which may affect some children.

Children who are hyposensitive or sensory seekers may not notice the smell of wee or poo if they are wet or soiled. Some may actively seek out strong smells, and sniff or play with bathroom products. They might enjoy the strong smell input of poo, and this may be linked to the rewards of smearing poo.

Gustatory

This provides information about different types of *taste* and is closely linked to smell.

The potential difficulties discussed in the previous paragraph may all have a similar impact. Some hyposensitive children may try to explore different substances to gain additional taste input, including attempting to eat soaps, toiletries or faeces.

Key sensory challenges and solutions

Children with autism will have different sensory needs that need to be analysed. A sensory profile is helpful in assessing these. This may be done by an occupational therapist or by using one of the other assessment tools discussed in the resources.

It is important to try and create a low arousal environment so the child feels more safe and secure. It can be quite difficult to differentiate the effects of the different senses on behaviour. Changes in the colour or texture of flooring or mats could impact on vision, balance or tactile sensation, and may lead to difficulties walking from, into or around the bathroom. If installing new equipment, such as hand-dryers, in bathrooms, it is vital to consider the sensory impact on the children who will be using them:

'We put new tiled flooring down in the bathroom at home and my seven-year-old son seemed to become stuck at the bathroom door and unable to enter. We put down a runner to the toilet and he happily crossed the threshold and used the toilet!'

It is important to consider the impact of sensory differences in the bathroom. There is an environmental sensory audit in the Practical Tools section to help with this.

Strategies for supporting a child may vary greatly and should be tailored for their individual needs.

Tactile, vestibular and proprioceptive challenges

These three systems are very closely linked, and will often need to be considered together. They are key areas to focus on regarding the impact of body sensation and positioning, balancing on the toilet, flooring within the bathroom, and wee, poo and nappies touching the body.

The child's understanding and awareness of body sensation and position will impact on problems encountered during toilet training and approaches to solve these:

- Is the toilet seat suitable? If necessary, experiment with an alternative shape or cover that gives a different tactile experience. A padded seat may feel softer and warmer.

- What is the most acceptable texture of toilet rolls or wipes?

- What is the right temperature for the bathroom, and how will this affect the toilet seat, floor or general environment?

- Is there a need for increased tactile input if this is what the child is seeking? See Chapter 15 on smearing for more ideas on this.

- Consider building in more opportunities for movement throughout the day to provide the additional input that may be needed by the proprioceptive, vestibular and tactile systems. Activities for maximising sensations received by the body may include bouncing on therapy balls, wheelbarrow walks, push-ups against walls, or things that they can fiddle with.

- Other resources to help with additional input include wobble cushions, bean-bags, and therabands on the back of chair legs which the child can kick against.

Difficulties with balance on the toilet:

'He always pushes himself right to the back of the toilet to try and feel secure – I now use a foam swim tube next to the cistern so he pushes himself onto that.'

- Use a toilet seat with a smaller hole.

- Install a handrail, on both sides if needed.

- Use a footstool (this is always a good idea!).

- Have feet marks on the floor or stool to show where the feet should go to ensure correct positioning and help them to know where to put their feet.

- Use a lap-pad to increase body awareness and help increase sensation from their legs through the pressure that is provided.

- Use a rolled-up towel or cut-up foam swim tube behind them to show them how far back they should sit and increase sensation and provide a feeling of security.

- Allow the child to squat on the toilet if that is their preference. They may need understanding and tolerance at school regarding this.

- Use a device that allows them to squat (see 'Squatty Potty' in the Resources section).

Flooring – stimulating balance, vision or temperature:

- Cover tiled or patterned flooring with a non-slip mat.

- Avoid having too many changes or varieties in colour or texture.

Limited awareness of body sensations – 'not feeling the need to go':

'I could never tell when I need to go to the toilet – so I taught myself to go when one of my friends goes.' *(Jill aged 23)*

- Use visual reminders, timers, phone alarms or a vibrating watch as an indicator to go to the toilet.

- For some children, let them go without pants for a short length of time in summer so they can see when they have a wee and learn to connect this sensation with themselves.

Limited awareness of wee or poo in nappy or pants:

- Use a nappy liner, pad or pants worn inside the nappy to increase awareness of wetness.

Anxiety about wee or poo touching or splashing on their body or clothes:

- Put a piece of toilet paper in the toilet before using it to reduce risk of splashes.

- Teach the child how far down to pull their trousers or pants.

- Let the child wear disposable gloves to avoid contact with wee or poo.

Liking the feeling of wee or poo in nappy or pants as this gives increased sensory input:

- Explore options to increase tactile sensory input in other ways, for example tightly fitting clothing or fiddle toys.

Liking the sensation of wearing a nappy – as it provides deep pressure increasing the sensations experienced:

- Allow the child to wear tight-fitting pants or shorts. For some children you may initially need to do this over the nappy.

- Provide deep pressure in other ways – using weighted lap-pads, blankets, massage or tight clothing.

- Gradually reduce the size or tightness of the nappy as the child gets more confident.

Visual input

Hypersensitive/sensory avoiders:

- Reduce the amount of visual information on the walls and think about the need for calming colours for walls and towels.

- Reduce the glare from lighting – small press-on lights or low wattage bulbs may be useful.

- Think about reflections, and whether mirrors need to be changed or removed.

- Let children wear sunglasses in the bathroom.

- Reduce visual overload by putting toiletries or equipment in boxes or out of the direct line of vision.

Hyposensitive/sensory seekers:

- Provide bright lighting.

- Provide visually stimulating input for the child to see, such as charts, pictures, cartoons, sensory lights or ceiling-mounted fiddle toys or mobiles.

Sounds

'The sound of the hand-dryer petrified him…until we realised that he never knew that it actually stopped…explaining how it worked helped him understand and manage his fear – he then wanted to stay and count how long it lasted before stopping!'

Hypersensitive/sensory avoiders:

- Use ear-defenders, earplugs or headphones for accessing some bathrooms, particularly public toilets.

- Use curtains, mats or towels to reduce the impact of echoes in the bathroom.

- Put a piece of toilet paper in the toilet prior to using it to decrease the sounds that weeing or pooing can make.

- If a child finds flushing distressing, record the sound of the flush and play it at varying intensities to gradually desensitise the child.

- Avoid bathrooms with hand-dryers if they are distressing.

Hyposensitive/sensory seekers:

- Provide alternative things to provide auditory input if this is what the child is seeking; for example musical toys with interesting sounds.

- For repetitive flushing, include a visual cue for a single flush followed by a different enjoyable activity. Having a 'finish' box to put the 'flush' cue in on completion may benefit some children.

Smells

Hypersensitive/sensory avoiders:

- Reduce smell input by using non-perfumed toiletries and cleaning products; think about detergents and fabric conditioners used on towels.

- Use odour neutralisers.

- Install an extractor device and ensure good ventilation.

- Allow a child to take something with them to sniff to distract from other smells.

Hyposensitive/sensory seekers:

- Increase smell input by using air-fresheners.

- Allow a child to have something with them to sniff to provide them with strong olfactory input, such as a wristband with perfume or essential oil, or scratch-and-sniff stickers.

- Build experiences of olfactory stimulation into their daytime routine.

Meeting sensory needs throughout the day

Reactions to sensation can be affected by stress, previous memories and experience. Many children also have difficulties with being at the right level of arousal or alertness for the situation they are in. They are often at the extreme ends of arousal, and never feeling 'just right'.

As well as examining the specific challenges associated with using the toilet, it can be helpful to build in a scheduled mixture of sensory input to a child's daily routine. The aim of this is to help their nervous system feel better organised and support the child's attention and performance through providing a mixture of calming, alerting and organising activities.

Calming activities

This will include activities which help to relax the nervous system, to help reduce anxiety, sensory defensiveness and sensory overload.

Examples include stress balls, fiddle toys, weighted items, rocking chair, soothing smells, low-level lighting, relaxing music, sleeping bags, blankets, cushions or deep pressure massage.

Alerting activities

Activities which are alerting to the nervous system help the child become more focused and attentive, and are particularly useful for those children who are under-responsive or passive.

Examples include bright lighting, loud music, strong smells, messy play, running games, ball bouncing, trampoline or stimulating sensory toys.

Organising activities

These will help with keeping the child's nervous system at the right level of stimulation, and allow them to be more focused and attentive.

Examples include movement activities such as pulling or pushing heavy objects, wheelbarrow walks, swimming, chewing or blowing, vibrating pillows, massagers or sitting on a physio ball.

In summary, it is always helpful to consider sensory differences, and these may coexist with other aspects of a child's autism, behaviour and general experiences. An evaluation of behaviour should always include a holistic consideration of a child's experiences and environment.

Suggestions to assist with assessing sensory differences and implementing strategies for supporting with these are included in the Resources section.

Chapter 14

AUTISM AND BEHAVIOUR

PROBLEM SOLVING

> To change your child's behaviour you need to be able to make
> sense of that behaviour, and making sense of your child's
> behaviour means making sense of the autism. *(Whitaker 2001)*

To make sense of difficult behaviours related to toilet training
and learning continence, it is essential to consider the underlying
reasons for them. These may be specific to the child's autism, but
other factors such as physical functioning and emotional stress
may be important. Some children may experience specific fears
and phobias linked to toilets, such as worrying that something will
come up from the toilet, falling in or being frightened by the noise
of hand-dryers.

Factors linked to autism that underlie problems in using the
toilet include a child's need for routine, rigidity and difficulties
in communication and social understanding. Any of these factors
can make it hard for the child to understand the world and learn
new skills.

It is first necessary to focus on exactly *what* a child is doing, in order to interpret the reasons *why* they are doing it, and then decisions can be made on *how* to approach it. This chapter will look at the following behaviours:

Not using the toilet to wee and poo:

- Refusing to wee in the toilet.

- Only pooing in a nappy.

- Weeing and pooing in the wrong place.

Using the toilet differently:

- Squatting on the toilet.

- Sitting the wrong way round on the toilet.

Transferring skills:

- Toilet trained in one environment – but not in others.

- Using different toilets.

Playing with toilets:

- Putting things down the toilet.

- Repeated flushing.

Toilet paper and how to use it properly:

- Unable to wipe themselves effectively.

Regression:

- A recurrence of problems using the toilet after a period of success.

Making sense of behaviour

When trying to make sense of behaviour, it is vital to try to understand the reason for this and the purpose it serves.

It can be helpful to use the concept of an iceberg, an idea originally developed by Division TEACCH and used by many today when looking at behaviour. The key principle is to consider any underlying factors in order to identify a reason for the behaviour.

We need to consider the behaviour that we observe, and then examine what might be the reasons for this. Possible explanations include the following: the child is trying to communicate; they do not understand what they are being asked to do; or they are gaining satisfaction and pleasure from the results of the behaviour.

There may be some circumstances where the observed behaviour is not related to difficulty in using the toilet, but is in response to other stresses the child is experiencing, including anxiety or changes in circumstances or environment. When toileting problems recur after achieving success, this may be caused by some kind of stress acting as a trigger factor.

This approach is described in a number of commonly used formulae, including the following:

ABC – Antecedent, Behaviour, Consequence

STAR – Settings, Triggers, Action, Response

PPP – Predisposing, Precipitating and Perpetuating factors.

The principle underlying each of these approaches is to progress from evaluating the factors causing the behaviour, to examining factors that are maintaining it, and then considering the consequences of the behaviour.

It is important to consider the individual features of a child's autism in order to evaluate the underlying reasons causing the difficulties with toilet training. These may include differences in communication, interaction, understanding and sensory processing.

The results or response that a child receives from their behaviour is vital to consider, and is often important in maintaining the behaviour. They may be engaging in the behaviour in order to achieve something. This could include achieving time on their own, which can also avoid less welcome activities or stressful demands. They may enjoy the reaction they see from those around them – if the adult gets angry or shouts, this can look like quite an exciting reaction to some children. An angry reaction may be providing predictability, as when people become angry their behaviour follows a more predictable pattern. There may be some children who are more comfortable with this than with receiving praise or excitement.

It is important to remember that children are usually not doing things just to annoy adults. If it appears that a child is deliberately doing something to achieve a reaction, it may be that the reaction itself is rewarding, and the behaviour is their form of communication about it.

When underlying factors causing the behaviour are understood, it is time to progress to make a plan to either teach a new behaviour, or enable them to continue the behaviour in a safer or more acceptable way.

In trying to change or adapt behaviour, it is always more successful when the alternative is easier for the children to achieve or provides them with a more satisfying result.

Problem solving

Not using the toilet to wee and poo

Children may refuse to use the toilet at all, or they may sit on it without using it and then wee and poo in the wrong place, on the floor, behind the door or somewhere else of their choosing!

If they have always used a nappy, and been changed in other rooms, they may have little understanding of what the toilet is for. They may associate either weeing or pooing (or both) with the places that they have become used to, and find changing this stressful. They may also have become used to certain body positions, for example crouching or standing when they wee and poo, and then they will find sitting on the toilet unfamiliar and uncomfortable, which will make it more difficult for them to let go of their wee and poo.

Confusion about what the bathroom is for can be a challenge for some children. If they have become accustomed to just using the bathroom for washing and bathing, they may find it difficult to make sense of being asked to go there for a wee and poo.

There are many products and alternative activities in the bathroom that may be distracting for a child, or more enjoyable, which can prevent them focusing on what they are supposed to be doing.

Many children have fears and anxiety about using the toilet or going into the bathroom. This may be linked to bright lighting, echoes, the feeling of water splashing on them when they use the toilet, or a fear of falling in.

Some of the following solutions may be helpful:

- Use visual timetables to help them understand the routine and sequences; any changes to these should be introduced gradually.

- Use a clear picture, or sequence of pictures, of the behaviour you are trying to teach.

- Link their original behaviour to any new routines they need to learn step by step.

- Ensure that the bathroom is a calm and comfortable place; things that may help for some children may be muted colours, gentle lighting, soft music, removing distractions and providing the child with calming toys or materials.

- Encourage the child to sit on the toilet long enough to relax, so they are more likely to be able empty their bowel and bladder.

- Review their seating position, use a toilet seat on which they feel safe and secure and provide additional physical support for balance if needed.

- Use feet marks on the floor to help them sit in the correct position.

- Ensure a good fluid intake to help bowel and bladder function.

- The sound of running water in the sink while the child is sitting on the toilet may encourage them to have a wee.

- It may be fun to show a child how to blow raspberries on the back of their hand or blow bubbles. This can sometimes help them with having a poo, as the actions involve the same muscles that are needed to push a poo out and it can also help them relax.

Children who need a nappy for pooing (and this is a common behaviour)

- All planning should involve the child as much as possible, and also all others who are involved in their life.

- To help children move from where they are currently having a poo to the toilet will often benefit from a staged approach.

- Consider ways to help the child feel familiar and comfortable when they are in the bathroom.

- Remember that children who ask for their nappy or go and find it when they want a poo have learnt how to recognise and respond to the sensation from their body.

- Encouraging a child to go into the bathroom to have a poo is an important early step, if necessary, while still using a nappy. Some children can use a mat or small rug to stand on when they are doing a poo in their nappy, and this can gradually be moved into the bathroom and nearer to the toilet.

- It is important to teach the child to sit on the toilet and become accustomed to this, with their nappy still on if needed.

- Once the child is comfortable sitting on the toilet, the next stage is to gradually reduce their reliance on their nappy. This might be achieved through using a single or combined strategy of loosening the nappy or reducing its size.

- Loosening the nappy may involve securing it less tightly each day, on a gradual basis. The nappy may eventually end up just being placed over the toilet seat and the child sits on it, before then moving onto the reducing size strategy.

- Reducing size might be done by cutting a hole in the nappy that eventually becomes big enough after several sessions for the poo to fall through. Alternatively, caregivers have tried cutting sections off the nappy to gradually reduce its size.

'We found a portable bidet which has been designed to be inserted into the toilet under the toilet seat. We've used this

to help children who still needed to sit on their nappy (the nappy then rested on this) and with children who were getting distressed by the fear of their poo dropping in the toilet.'
(Continence nurse)

Weeing or pooing in the wrong place

- A staged approach is needed to gradually move them from the place they are currently using, towards the toilet.

- Visual cues or symbols should be used as needed to help understanding.

- Some children may be helped by putting a potty or commode in the place they currently use, and then gradually moving this into the bathroom, nearer the toilet, and eventually being able to sit down on the toilet.

> Sam would only go to the bottom of the garden under a tree to have a poo. The first step to change this was to put a potty underneath him, and then a toilet-tent over him. The potty and tent were gradually moved up the garden towards the house, eventually getting him to use the downstairs toilet. Visual supports were used to reinforce what he was being asked to do (it did take a very long time!).

Using the toilet differently

Western-style toilets are designed to be used by sitting on them and facing to the front, and most people naturally understand this. Some children may not realise that this is how they should be used, and if they are sitting or squatting on them differently then they may be happy with this. Many people find using a different style of toilet on holiday very challenging, and it useful to think about this when considering the difficulties experienced by people with autism.

Children may sit facing the toilet cistern so they can hold on and feel safer.

Other children may prefer to squat on top of the toilet seat, which, interestingly, is a more natural position in which to have a poo. Some children may find this an easier position in which to use the toilet, especially if there is a history of constipation.

Sometimes children are trying to increase their sensory input (sensory seekers) and may find that squatting provides strong vestibular and proprioceptive input.

It may be necessary to balance social conventions with the child's needs and preferences. Some children may be able to gradually learn how to sit on a toilet, and become accustomed to it:

- Use a visual image to demonstrate the conventional seating position.

- Place feet marks on the floor to help with body positioning.

- Introduce the idea of changing sitting position using a Social Story™ to explain why people sit on the toilet facing the front.

- Discuss with the child which toilets they can use to start practising sitting down on. If necessary, you may need to reach a compromise. This could mean using school toilets in the expected way, but following their preferences at home.

- Introduce a Squatty Potty. This is a footstool that sits around the toilet and enables the toilet to be used in a squatting position.

- Review whether the child needs a programme of movement-related activities to provide them with additional vestibular and proprioceptive input.

- Consider an alternative toilet seat, rails and a footstool to aid with feeling balanced and secure.

- Provide physical supports to help with feeling more secure; for example, a foam swim tube or rolled-up towel next to the cistern to lean back onto.

Difficulties with transferring skills

> ## MYTH
>
> ### Refusing to use other toilets is just a child being stubborn

Key difficulties can include being fully toilet trained in one setting but not another. A child may prefer using one particular toilet and be reluctant to use others, especially public toilets.

Underlying reasons for this can include a child having difficulty transferring their learning from one place to another. This may mean that they will need to be taught specifically how to use the toilet in the other settings they access (it is helpful to use the same strategies).

If a child is toilet trained in one environment but not another, it is important to consider the factors that operate successfully where they *are* using the toilet, and how these can be transferred to the different settings. Good communication and analysis are essential. Some children find it easier to learn toileting skills at home as it can be a more familiar and relaxed environment.

The structured nature of school or residential services with programmed timetables and can facilitate learning in that setting for some children. At times, potential differences in approaches from staff members may make it confusing.

> One staff member who sat the child on the toilet every time the nappy was changed discovered after some time that another member of staff just changed the nappy, and didn't ask the child to go anywhere near the toilet!

Public toilets are often a source of great anxiety for many people, not just those with autism. The potential differences in sensory processing experienced by children with autism can make unpleasant smells and noises perceived more intensely so they are more distressing. The need for familiarity and structure can also make accessing new environments particularly challenging:

- If possible, it is important to encourage children to use different toilets when toilet training is beginning in order to prevent future rigidity.

- Identify what factors contribute to success in the environment where they are using the toilet successfully.

- Implement the same or similar approaches in other environments, using the same visual structure, language, prompts and supplies.

- Some children may benefit from using the same type of toilet roll, wet wipes or portable toilet seat in all environments, to help with transferring skills and making them feel safe and secure. Any extra equipment should be gradually phased out as the child becomes accustomed to different settings.

- Some children may find it easier to accept change linked to something else they understand, such as changing class or age. Good preparation for this is necessary.

- Introduce practice sessions for going into different toilets; initially this may be only to walk in and not to actually use the toilet.

- Acknowledge fears and anxieties and teach the child strategies they can use for self-calming. These could include slow deep breathing or visualisation.

- Allowing a child to wear ear-defenders or sunglasses can reduce the sensory impact of a new environment.

- Make sure there are suitable accessible toilets that are clean and quiet. Accessible toilets in the UK can be accessed with a RADAR[11] Key and may be quieter and less overwhelming.

- Explain to the child about public toilets, and why and how people need to use them.

---

11 www.radar.org.uk

'We made Sarah a "toilet inspector" and this eventually helped her being able to use some public toilets. Her task was to just go into the toilets and give them a score out of 10. We then discussed which, if any, toilets on her rating scale she would be able to use, and she agreed she could try those she had rated as 9 or 10.'

Playing with the toilet!

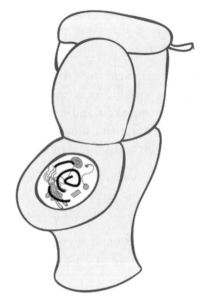

Children may not understand what the toilet is for, and often find many more interesting things to do with it than use it for wees and poos! Posting things down the toilet or repeatedly flushing it can be far more enjoyable for the child than doing what the adults want them to do. In addition, the bathroom may be a very exciting environment to explore, especially if they enjoy playing with water or toiletries.

When children enjoy putting the wrong things down the toilet, some people have reduced this behaviour by putting a box next to the toilet with interesting things that the child can post into the box. This is reinforced by visual supports on the box and on the toilet, indicating what should go where.

Woodcock and Page (2010) discuss a family who reduced the child's desire for throwing toilet rolls out of the bathroom window by providing ribbons attached to a piece of wood on the window sill. The child had fun throwing the ribbons out of the window and watching them fall to the ground. This replaced the frustration the parents felt at finding all the toilet rolls outside and still met the child's need for this activity and enjoyment!

- Use clear visual cues to explain what should be done in the bathroom, for example washing their hands in the basin.

- Put time for similar activities that achieve the same effect for the child onto their timetable, for example water play and bubbles.

- Use a picture of acceptable activities with a green tick to indicate that they are ok; and use a red cross to indicate when they should not be done in the bathroom.

- If a child keeps flushing the toilet, put this on a visual routine to help them understand the right time to do this.

- Have one 'flushing' card to give the child when it is time to flush the toilet, putting it in the 'finish box' when the action is completed.

Toilet paper and how to use it properly

Key difficulties can include being unable to wipe themselves effectively after using the toilet, being reluctant to use toilet paper or having difficulty in judging the correct amount to use.

Underlying reasons for these problems can include a child not understanding what they should do, why they need to do this and the implications of not wiping properly.

They may find the physical act of wiping difficult, particularly if they have motor coordination problems. The toilet roll may feel uncomfortable, especially if they have tactile sensitivity. A child who has fear and anxiety about germs and contamination may find the idea of putting their hand anywhere close to their poo particularly distressing. An inability to wipe themselves can be one of the underlying causes of smearing poo.

The following may be helpful:

- Include a picture or symbol on the visual schedule that shows wiping.

- Introduce some physical practice sessions on wiping, and try to make this fun. Initially it can include learning to wipe something they can see, such as jam or paint.

- Learning to twist to wipe behind may be helped by introducing fun activities to teach this skill. An example could be a game where you 'tuck a tail' into the back of a child's trousers so they can then practise reaching behind them to grab the tail!

- Explain to a child why and how they need to wipe, breaking the task down and using rules or Social Stories™. Explanations work better if they are very visual, perhaps using a picture of clean toilet roll to show them when they have done this properly.

- Physically guide a child's hand to help them wipe themselves and learn how to do it.

- Provide toilet paper or wipes that are easy to use. Consider what colour, texture, smell and temperature the child will like.

- Explain how many sheets of paper should be used or put a mark on the wall to show how far the toilet roll should be pulled down.

- Restrict the child's access to the number of tissues or wipes that will be needed.

- If a child has extreme germ or contamination anxieties, the use of disposable gloves may be helpful.

Regression and relapses
The first thing is not to panic. There can be a recurrence of problems with wetting in the day or at night, or with bowel control. Any of the problems described above may occasionally recur.

It is vital to consider whether there are any specific physical problems present, such as constipation. This may be linked to bedwetting, soiling difficulties and reluctance to use the toilet. It needs to be identified promptly and treated.

As well as ensuring that specific health problems have been considered and treated if necessary, it is essential to look at other factors which may have contributed to this change in behaviour. Causal factors can include changes in routines and associated anxiety. Alteration in family dynamics such as a new baby, moving house or family stresses may be triggers. School life is often changing, and this may include alterations in staff, classroom, playground or timetables. Children with autism can be vulnerable and experience bullying, and it can be difficult for them to understand and explain what is happening. Any of these difficulties can lead to a child trying to regain some control over their environment; the toileting behaviour a child is displaying may be their only way of regaining some control and communicating their distress.

It is essential to address factors causing anxiety or stress. Making life more predictable for a child will be helpful to increase their feelings of security and being in control.

It is essential to recognise the needs of families and caregivers. They will benefit from continuing support with trying to manage behaviour and reassurance that things will resolve, although it may take time.

It is important to address toileting problems as behaviour, and try to remove any feelings of guilt carers have, as this can interfere with achieving a positive outcome.

TOP TIPS

1. Observe where and when a particular behaviour is occurring.

2. Identify the triggers underlying the behaviour.

3. Remember, there may be more than one cause for a behaviour.

4. Explore if there is a possibility of any physical health problems present.

5. Look at whether the difficulty is related to their autism.

6. Remember, changes in behaviour may take time, but improve with careful analysis and an appropriate plan that is implemented consistently.

Chapter 15

SMEARING

CAUSES AND SOLUTIONS

Poo art!

In 2014 at the Tate Modern there was a large exhibition by Richard Hamilton. He was described in the exhibition guide as 'One of the most important and influential artists of the twentieth century'. One of his large paintings from the early 1980s entitled *The Citizen* included IRA prisoners taking part in dirty protests, smearing the walls of their cells with faeces. The exhibition guide said that Richard Hamilton suggested these were wall paintings. Children also sometimes smear poo on walls and other places, and while this is rarely artistic, it often gives dramatic expression of their emotions: anger, frustration and sometimes curiosity.

The discovery of poo smeared on walls, behind the fridge door, on the carpet, bedding or anywhere unexpected is one of the most distressing situations for parents and carers connected with toileting:

'I didn't know this happened to other people. I've never told anyone about this before, as I thought it was all my fault and they'd think I was a bad parent, and they'd take her away and put her in care.' *(Parent of an eight-year-old girl)*

It is vital to be sensitive in discussing this behaviour, as it is always upsetting for families. It is important to avoid blaming the child or the family.

Smearing poo can happen at home, school or other places. It can occur with any child, including those with autism. The triggers that initiate it are varied, and there may be different reasons for the behaviour continuing. These may include the rewards of producing a significant adult reaction or the time and attention given following the episode. Negative reactions are often as satisfying as positive ones:

> 'Every time he soiled and smeared poo it was so bad I had to put him in the bath. After a few weeks it was getting worse, and I realised how much he enjoyed soaking in the warm water. I changed and gave him a quick shower without talking, and the behaviour improved in a week or two.' *(Parent of a ten-year-old boy)*

Effective intervention and management for smearing illustrate the themes of this book. It is necessary to think about the impact of autistic, emotional and physical aspects, and how these may interact to cause or maintain the problem.

There is often an underlying reason for smearing; this may be physical difficulties with wiping, or unsuccessful attempts to deal with sticky poo and constipation. It may be linked to a need for sensory stimulation, or a repetition of enjoyable experiences.

Understanding what to do with poo

Smearing behaviour in some children may be simply because they do not understand what to do with their poo, particularly if it happens to get into their hands after opening their bowels. In some children, it occurs because they sit on the toilet, have a poo, and then there is nobody immediately available to help them, and they do not know what to do next. There may be a need to explore the availability of prompt help for the child to resolve this difficulty.

Strategies include using a toilet training routine with words or pictures that clearly explain each step of the process using visual picture sequences or Social Stories™. Changing the child promptly helps to reduce the opportunities for smearing and increases their experience of being clean. Increased supervision during toilet breaks can help avoid the behaviour and can be a teaching opportunity.

Underlying emotional factors

It is important to consider whether emotional factors are causing or maintaining smearing behaviour. These may include curiosity, boredom, distress, anxiety, anger, depression or the effects of abuse. The fact that smearing almost invariably produces a strong adult reaction may be very rewarding for a child. For other children, reactions may increase their anxiety or anger. There may be a need to consider the family dynamics and any factors causing stress, especially considering the potential stress levels in families who have a child with autism.

Smearing faeces is a behaviour that is highly distressing for everyone involved with the child. There is an increased amount of cleaning and washing, as well as emotional distress and exhaustion in the caregivers. If the child does this behaviour in public, it will significantly increase this stress. Families may be reluctant to discuss smearing and seek help with it as they feel they might be criticised.

In trying to assess and manage the smearing behaviour, and identify any causative emotional factors, observation and input from those who know the child and family well are needed. Additional assessment by an independent professional such as a family therapist or psychologist may be helpful to explore and understand these causative factors and suggest interventions. The initial approach to smearing caused by emotional difficulties is to address this stress first and provide support to families. As emotional issues are resolved, the smearing may reduce without other intervention.

Smearing poo invariably produces a strong adult reaction that may be very satisfying. This response may contribute to the behaviour continuing. It is usually best to avoid scolding or punishment as this does not help, but may increase the stress for all.

It may be necessary to completely remove any reaction to the smearing behaviour, alongside increasing reactions to other more acceptable behaviours. Some parents have found that a matter-of-fact response together with encouraging the child to help with cleaning the mess may help, especially if this means that the child has less time for things they enjoy doing. However, when a child is encouraged to help with cleaning it is important that this is a learning strategy, not a punishment.

Physical or sexual abuse may need to be considered in some cases linked to soiling and smearing behaviours. If this is a possibility, detailed evaluation of risks and vulnerability of the child and their needs should follow safeguarding guidelines and local child protection policies. This will be followed by appropriate planning and intervention for their future needs and security.

Sensory rewards of the behaviour

There may be sensory satisfaction for the child. Poo is smelly and warm and they may like the strong aroma and tactile feeling of the manipulation of this interesting squidgy stuff.

A sensory profile can be helpful in understanding sensory aspects of this behaviour, and a programme to provide alternative sensory stimulation may reduce the need for seeking input through smearing. Introducing increased sensory input throughout the day, or providing easy access to alternative forms of stimulation may be helpful. Suitable clothing such as Houdini suits or onesies may restrict a child's access to their poo and help in reducing or eliminating this behaviour.

Potential alternative forms of sensory input as part of a structured timetable or offered as a visual alternative to smearing could include:

- Play-dough activities with warm dough

- Finger painting

- Sand and water play, shaving foam

- Hand massage with warm cream

- Squeeze balls

- Strong smell input; using diffusers, hankies with strong scents on, strong-smelling stickers.

Body awareness and coordination

Some children who are showing smearing behaviour may actually be trying to wipe and clean themselves inefficiently. They may not be sure exactly where to wipe, or how to do it effectively. It may be necessary to teach them how to do this, perhaps using dolls, diagrams or pictures.

A holiday project at home with eye shadow drawn round the anus and rewards for success in wiping it off may be a fun way to teach this.

Quite a number of children with autism may have coordination difficulty in twisting and getting their hand into the right place for cleaning themselves. They may find it helpful to be taught the sequence of movements and practise this. Making it into a fun game such as 'twist and turn' can make it easier to learn. Advice from a physiotherapist may be helpful.

Putting a bean bag into a pocket at the bottom of their back can be a fun game to help teach the movements needed.

Constipation and overflow soiling

In Chapter 12 we discussed constipation and soiling. Smearing may be a result of this, because constipated poo is sticky and difficult to wipe. The constipated child may not have awareness of when their bowels are going to open, and overflow leaking followed by soiling accidents may occur. This may result in the child trying unsuccessfully to clean themselves after unexpectedly finding poo in their underwear.

Children who are constipated often find that the poo may take a long time to come out and it is hard to successfully empty their bowel. The child may get bored and leave the toilet too soon, so the poo arrives in the wrong place, such as the bathroom floor. The arrival of poo soon after leaving the toilet suggests that the bowel has not fully emptied, even if there has been some success in the toilet.

There may be a need to monitor the bowel pattern, and consider the effectiveness of bowel emptying. If needed, discuss the benefits of medication to obtain more effective bowel actions that fully empty the large bowel.

Soiling in the night

Probably one of the worst ways to start the day is with a dirty, smelly child and soiled bedding. Children don't purposely smear poo just to upset adults, but they may find the smearing experience very satisfying.

It is often caused when children hold the poo in all day, sometimes because they are afraid of emptying their bowels in the toilet. They may be too busy to go to the toilet and so postpone this. At bedtime, the bowel is full and when the child falls asleep and relaxes, they are unable to continue holding the poo in. The bowel then leaks or empties either into a nappy or nightwear. This will often wake the child, either at the time, or afterwards, and they may then explore what has happened, and try to remove it. Some children may find this a pleasurable experience, and may not understand how distressing it is for everybody else.

Approaches to this problem will include ensuring effective daytime bowel emptying. This can be helped with healthy eating and increased fluids. A small amount of laxative to help ensure that the bowel is opened during the day may help to resolve the problem. If the bowels are fully emptied in the day, there will not be night-time accidents. A toilet timetable with reminders to try to have a poo before bed can help. Bath-time can be relaxing and sitting on the toilet after this may be a good time to try. There are back-closing clothes and pyjamas that may be helpful at times to manage night-time soiling episodes.

Causes of and responses to smearing

Causes	Response
Constipation	Treat and manage
Inability to wipe effectively	Teach skills
Motor skills and coordination	Assess skills and arrange for further assessment if needed
Sensory stimulation or enjoyment	Offer alternatives
Psychological stress, anxiety and family emotional difficulties	Assess and refer to a specialist service if needed. Support and help to provide predictability, stress management, and relaxation
Enjoys the response of others	Modify the responses
Curiosity	Reduce response and encourage help in cleaning. Provide other activities to explore

Chapter 16

COMPLIANCE DIFFICULTIES AND PATHOLOGICAL DEMAND AVOIDANCE (PDA)

'I can't get him to cooperate, he doesn't seem bothered.'

'Why don't children do what we want them to, when it would make things better for everyone?'

Many parents say such things and it is always very helpful to try to understand the dynamics of this difficulty, and it is essential to try to gain an insight into the child's perspective. There is usually a reason for any child's behaviour, and this is especially relevant for children with autism. Understanding underlying reasons for a child's lack of cooperation with toileting programmes which may be causing conflict is essential in addressing this and engaging the child constructively.

Possible causes and responses
The child doesn't understand what they are being asked:

- We may need to explain more simply and use clear language, signs or objects of reference.

We are asking the child to do something too complicated:

- We may need to break down the task into easier stages with a simple initial target.

The child has become comfortable with the way they have become used to:

- We may need to think about strategies to achieve change, and make it feel safe and less threatening. We can focus on the advantages for the child, targets and fun rewards.

The child prefers to do something else:

- This may be logical. We may need to consider whether we are asking at the right time, or how to help the child learn alternative priorities.

They do not remember until afterwards:

- We could think about prompts to create fun reminders, and evaluate organisation and sequencing skills that may be difficult for some children.

The child may have developed excellent skills in avoiding instructions and requests:

- Don't we all do this? Maybe we need to think about a novel approach that interests the child and use good motivators.

The child is too worried and anxious to learn a new skill at present:

- We may need to help with these feelings before starting making new demands on the child.

The child needs to feel in control:

- Adults control everything in a child's life: what they do, where they go and how they do it. Deciding where to do your wee or poo is one of the few things that adults often cannot control. It may help to give children other things to control, such as what they do after they go to the toilet. It is helpful to reduce and avoid conflict as much as possible.

The child may not have the same sensations from their body that we expect:

- This is really interesting. We all can block out feelings that make us uncomfortable and avoid thinking about things we haven't done or mistakes we have made. Children may be very good at this and genuinely not notice and appreciate wet or dirty pants or puddles. Children with autism may not be as aware of their body signals as other people. They may also have constipation, which may stretch the bowel and reduce the sensation.

There may be a combination of many of the above:

- We need to think carefully about what the child understands and feels. It is often helpful to ask them (adults often don't do this!).

- They have Pathological Demand Avoidance syndrome. They may have many of the above, but display oppositional behaviour in an extreme form.

The conclusion for all of these causes and responses is that to be successful adults need to understand the child's perspective and adapt their approach the problem to make it easier for the child. It is part of the role of the adult to be able to analyse and understand situations, and devise appropriate solutions.

Pathological Demand Avoidance Syndrome (PDA)

This is a relatively new diagnostic category in the autism spectrum and is becoming increasingly used as a way of understanding the difficulties that a group of children may have. It may need an assessment from professionals with experience of this to identify these children and to help create appropriate strategies to help with their toileting.

Children with PDA display a significant avoidance of everyday demands. They see situations where demands may be placed on them as particularly stressful and anxiety-provoking and use avoidance as a way of coping. There are a number of ways in which they may be similar to or different from children with more classic autism. Characteristics include some apparently good social skills (although these tend to be superficial) and very high anxiety levels (which aren't necessarily apparent or expressed conventionally).

There has been debate among professionals about the understanding of this condition as a diagnostic label. In dealing with problems of learning toileting skills, avoidance and oppositional behaviour is frequently found, and responds to some of the ideas described for children with PDA.

Elizabeth Newson (1998) described how generally accepted strategies that are advocated for working for children with autism and Asperger syndrome were not proving successful for children with PDA.

How compliance difficulties may affect strategies for toilet training

- Refusal to eat, drink or take medication; this is often part of the demand avoidance pattern.

- The problems of using rewards; children with PDA may 'see through' the use of rewards to encourage them. Be cautious about rewarding success: although praise can be motivating, it may make the child decide not to give in so easily next time. Rewards may be an area for negotiation and argument.

- Difficulty in negotiating; children's anxiety levels are so high that negotiating is a particular challenge.

- Changing the boundaries and rules; children with PDA can be especially committed to following their own agenda and trying to make others do this too.

- Anxiety and control; this is a key part of these children's profile and the toilet is often an area of conflict.

- Family stress; these children are often extremely challenging and accurate diagnosis can be difficult and may only be made later, compounding understanding of the child and appropriate strategies being implemented.

- Lack of understanding from family members, friends, other professionals and the public, in supermarkets, shops, playgrounds, and so on.

Many children with demand avoidance learn to behave in a compliant and tolerant way at school, but can display much worse behaviour at home. It is important to realise that this is not to do with less competent handling at home, and much more to do with the *limits* of the child's tolerance and the need to 'let their hair down' somewhere; if not understood, this can cause great tension between parents and teachers.

Newson (1998) has described some examples of avoidance behaviour:

- *Distracting adults:* 'Look out of the window!', 'I've got you a flower!', 'I love your necklace!', 'I'm going to be sick'.

- *Acknowledging demand but excusing self:* 'I'm sorry, but I can't', 'I'm afraid I've got to do this first', 'I'd rather do this', 'I don't have to, you can't make me'.

- *Physically demonstrating avoidance:* hides under table, curls up in corner, goes limp, dissolves into tears, drops everything, seems unable to look in the direction of the toilet (though retains eye contact).

- *Withdrawing into fantasy play:* talks only to doll or to other objects; appeals to doll, 'My girls won't let me do that', 'My teddy doesn't like this game'.

- *Doesn't engage in conversation about demand:* bombards adult with speech (or noises such as humming) to drown out demands or refuses to speak.

- *(As last resort)* Outbursts, screaming, hitting, kicking. This is best viewed as a display of distress. Occasionally, a child will find that they can produce maximum disruption, coupled with withdrawal of demands, by pulling his/her pants down, urinating on the floor, or some form of sexualised behaviour.

Useful strategies

It is important to have a flexible and imaginative approach to the child, and this may need to be very individual. It is helpful to know that what works today may not work tomorrow (because the child doesn't want to be caught out twice!), but that it may well work again in a week's time. Nothing will *invariably* work; it is helpful to have a *variety* of strategies available and not be too concerned if a particular one is unsuccessful on a particular day. Many routines that work well for children with classic autism or Asperger syndrome will be unsuccessful with this group.

It is important that children's avoidance behaviours should not be successful and distract adults. It is important to try to remain calm, paying the least possible attention to the behaviour, and continue to try to complete the task in progress without fuss:

- Give the child options (both of which achieve the goal): which toilet would you like to use; red or blue pants today.

- Try to empower him/her by allowing more choice in activities. A very useful strategy is to offer a choice of two activities in which the one you really want followed is the easier.

Jo refused to eat any vegetables or fruit, which made him more likely to be constipated. His support worker gave him the choice of cutting out shapes from cucumber, carrots and melons to eat in 'either a flower or a fish'. Jo liked to eat his shapes (although he wouldn't do this at home).

- Offer opportunities with no direct instruction and leave the response to the child's curiosity.

- Prioritisation; choose your battles to focus on the essential ones.

- Avoid confrontation; aim to be less directive and be prepared to negotiate compliance.

- As far as possible try to ignore negative behaviours, and keep calm.

- It is very common for a child with demand avoidance to resist social demands by lashing out or pushing forcefully, and sometimes by screaming or swearing. It is helpful to think of this behaviour as anxiety and not as aggression. It may be more appropriate to react in a reassuring way, instead of blaming or being angry.

- Use a variety of pace and presentation when asking. The use of more complex language may capture interest and has a less confrontational feel.

- Try to avoid direct verbal commands. You may find that making demands in an indirect way is often more successful. For example, 'I wonder what's the best way of getting this poo done – I can't quite think how to do it…' rather than the more directive 'Go to the toilet please.' If you have difficulty doing this, it may be helpful to tape-record and listen to your requests critically, and then practise rewording them to be more indirect.

- Include requests as part of normal conversation.

- Depersonalise demands by using other cues, for example timers or alarms.

- Disguise your expectations and be flexible, creative and sometimes unpredictable: 'pulling the rabbit out of the hat'. Try new ideas, and if a strategy doesn't work first time don't abandon it it may work on another occasion.

- Try to use variety and humour. You can coax, cajole and even challenge if you do so humorously: 'I bet you can't…' On occasions disguise your expectations of the child.

- Plan for an 'escape route' or 'bolthole' so that the child can withdraw at times of high anxiety.

- Role-play and pretending are often favoured by the child. Use role-play to your advantage; for instance, when trying to get the child to understand your point of view, get the child to take a turn as the parent or teacher.

- Use puppets and toy animals as a 'third person' to diffuse confrontation.

PART 5

WHAT NEXT?

Chapter 17

OLDER CHILDREN AND TEENAGERS

Growing up is often a difficult time, presenting new challenges. For children with autism the increasing social and educational demands are often especially difficult to manage. It is a time of life where young people are seeking their identity, planning their future and often struggling to develop their self-esteem.

We do not want to limit the possibility for children's potential, but we need to recognise that teenagers with autism may continue to need support and may have difficulty in taking age-appropriate responsibility.

MYTH

There's no point trying toilet training once they've hit adolescence or adulthood

The principles of planning, preparation and problem solving will apply equally to older children's toilet training. It is never too late to start toilet training.

For some there may be a need to focus and develop initial steps, while others may need to consolidate skills already learned. There will be some specific areas that are important to consider as children with autism are growing up:

Independence

The essential objective for every young person is to work towards maximising their independence. The teenage years are a period of continuing changes and development, demanding ongoing evaluation, reflection and adaptations if needed. Good preparation, planning and support are essential components of this and young people should be included and have a key role.

New settings

If young people are considering further education or a residential placement, it is vital to provide the resources and facilities to manage any continuing continence difficulties. Where children have the capacity, it is in their interests for them to take increasing responsibility for self-management of any continuing problems with bowel and bladder control. For some, continued support may be essential.

Young people should always be involved in planning for change, and good communication with detailed information about their continence needs will be needed.

Physical changes growing up

The onset of periods is daunting and young people need appropriate support and information. If at all possible, it is a significant advantage to have resolved any toilet training difficulties before menstruation commences. However, it can also be an important milestone which will help young people understand the importance of using the toilet and can motivate them to do this.

Many young people with learning disabilities will need additional support to help them understand the changes that are occurring and how to deal with them appropriately. This support may include teaching the young person the difference between wee, poo and periods, and the different approaches and resources for managing these. Input will need to be individualised to the child's level of understanding.

Toilet etiquette

Understanding toilet etiquette is important for all and can become more complex to understand during the teenage years and into adulthood. This is rarely taught explicitly to young people, and children with autism may not pick it up from their peer group.

This may be particularly relevant for boys, especially when using public toilets. Boys with autism will be less likely to work out the unspoken rules of using toilets and urinals, such as avoiding eye contact, no talking and the correct urinal to use (you're not supposed to stand next to someone else – you should leave a gap if possible!). There are YouTube clips and internet blogs to help explain some of these rules, along with apps to practise making the correct choices. The choice between a toilet cubicle or urinal may need to be discussed. Toilet training is frequently led by females, who may not be aware of the complexities of male toilet etiquette.

Girls may also need input to develop their understanding of protocol in public toilets to enable them to be more independent. There are now some books written for teenagers to help with this (e.g. Reynolds 2014a, 2014b). The rules for girls are very different from those for boys. It can be a much more sociable activity, with going to the toilet in a group of friends seen as normal, and potentially the visit to the toilet can be linked to sharing gossip, cigarettes and make-up as well as using the toilet.

Taking responsibility

There may be demands placed on some adolescents to take more responsibility for their toileting or taking their medication which some of them may not be ready for, or unwilling to do.

It is vital to be aware that chronological age is not necessarily the best indicator of readiness for increased responsibility. An adolescent's level of learning disability and any executive functioning difficulties must be taken into account. Of equal importance is their motivation to be responsible. All adolescents often need prompts and reminders; however, it may be a good opportunity to discuss a planned approach to reducing these and giving the young person more control and responsibility:

'My daughter has alarms set on her mobile at certain times to prompt her to go to the toilet.' *(Parent of a teenage girl)*

Giving young people responsibility for the management of any chronic condition is often problematic, and difficulties of adherence to treatment regimes have been discussed in relation to many chronic conditions. These difficulties are not surprising as young people often feel angry about having a problem needing treatment. One of the consistent features of adolescents with chronic health difficulties is that their condition often becomes poorly controlled at this time. This may impact on children at an important time in their life, and when plans are being made for their future.

Experience reveals that there is significant noncompliance with self-administered medication in a range of chronic conditions including diabetes, cancer and kidney disease. Noncompliance transcends the boundary of disease categories and age group. However, this is most prevalent during the adolescent years when the process of transition from parental dependency to autonomy produces confusion as to who is responsible for administration of medication.

A universal teenage reluctance to manage conditions and follow adult rules applies just as much to children with autism managing their continence difficulties and taking any medications. In addition, some young people may feel extremely negative about their autism and the impact this has on their life.

It is useful to consider the many reasons why a young person with autism may not take their medication reliably. This may include difficulties with routine, dislike of taking medication, reluctance to acknowledge the need for continued tablets or medicine, or just being fed up with it. A reduction in parental supervision, increased demand on the young person to take responsibility for their own treatment, eating and drinking, can all interact and lead to difficulties in maintaining reliable control of bowel and bladder difficulties. This can result in the bowel and bladder difficulties re-emerging or being less well controlled, and sometimes going haywire, but we should not give up!

'My son now uses a timer on his phone to tell him when to take his tablet.' *(Parent of a teenage boy)*

Reviewing bowel and bladder conditions

As children grow, their requirements for medication and the doses can often change. The treatment needed to control bowel or bladder conditions should be reviewed. Eating and drinking patterns in teenagers often change and most people rarely stick to healthy eating and often do not have the food and fluid that they know is ideal. Routines can also be influenced by peer group activities, social and sporting interests, and anxiety. The adolescent growth spurt will also affect the amount of medication required. All these factors can affect bowel patterns and regularity.

The educational and social demands on teenagers may create changes and these may impact upon their toileting patterns. The changes involved in adolescence are difficult for all young people but can be harder to manage for those with autism who struggle with change.

There is often a need for reassessment and extensive dialogue to engage with teenagers and provide appropriate support. They may need help to understand their toileting difficulty and why it occurs. It can be a good strategy to get the young person to evaluate the advantages of having good control, and to keep their own record of their progress. Many young people like to use gadgets, so electronic alarms and watches may be useful for them. There are several apps that use the Bristol Stool Form Scale which can be used to create a graph to track bowel function.

Relapses in bowel or bladder control

Most young people who learn bowel and bladder control usually retain this skill. Occasionally, though, there may be a relapse and recurrence of bowel and bladder problems. This can be upsetting and worrying for the young person and their friends and family. It is important to investigate the causes of this before beginning treatment or retraining. Relapses may be triggered by stress or changes in routine, or could be a new problem developing. The strategies and treatment for older children will need to be adapted for their maturity and growth.

Problems with bladder control

This can be caused by infection, which is more common in girls, and may be triggered by sexual activity. Advice needs to be provided about intimate hygiene in a way that can be understood by the young person. This needs to be specifically tailored for boys and girls.

Stress incontinence describes urinary leakage associated with coughing or laughing. It is uncommon in children, but can occur in older girls. It is more commonly linked to the strain on the pelvic muscles that occurs during pregnancy and childbirth.

Problems with bowel control

In teenagers this is most likely to be caused by constipation. This may be a recurrence of an earlier difficulty, but can appear as a new problem. It will improve with prompt treatment, but progress will need to be monitored to ensure that treatment has been effective and check if there is any need to use maintenance medication to prevent recurrence.

Inflammation of the large bowel, especially with diarrhoea or abdominal pain, could be an indicator of other conditions, including ulcerative colitis or Crohn's disease, which may have its onset in young people. Therefore the onset of any new bowel difficulties needs a medical assessment with appropriate advice.

Sexuality

Sexuality is an intrinsic part of personal identity which is expressed in a variety of ways, including thoughts, attitudes, values and behaviours (World Health Organisation 2006[12]). Sexuality can encompass anything from sexual acts, gender roles, expression of sexual feelings and fantasies, to same-sex relationships (Reynolds 2014b).

Children learn about sexuality through a combination of growing up, learning from their peers, observing what other people around them do, and structured sex education. Children with

---

12   www.who.int/reproductivehealth/topics/sexual_health/sh_definitions/en/

autism may fail to relate to much of this, therefore may need individualised and developmentally appropriate input.

It may be necessary to explain carefully to boys the difference between ejaculation and weeing. There is a range of specific material available for sex education for children with disabilities.

Why are we talking about this in a toileting book?

A common issue that gives rise to most concern is children touching their genital areas and masturbation. People often raise this as a concern in relation to toilet training when it is a behaviour that occurs as soon as the nappy is removed. Reluctance to take off the nappy will contribute to difficulties and lack of opportunity to learn to use the toilet. This is not a reason to keep a young person in nappies or prevent toilet training taking place.

Understanding and exploring your body is a natural and normal part of life. When a young person with autism is openly exploring their body, and is unaware that this should be a private activity, it can cause concern for parents and caregivers.

In some children, self-stimulation may be an indicator that they are ready to come out of nappies as they may be enjoying the relief at the feeling of not wearing a nappy. In other children, it may be the only opportunity they have to explore and learn about their own body, and the pleasure this can bring.

Masturbating is a normal activity and is only a problem when it occurs in front of other people or in the wrong place. It is an area that many people are reluctant to discuss. People's attitudes towards it may be influenced by their religious and moral beliefs. For any parent, indications of their child developing as a sexual person are uncomfortable; and if a child has a disability, this can give rise to additional concerns about their potential vulnerability.

Understanding and teaching about sexuality and masturbation needs to take into account the developmental level of the child and their physical and sexual needs.

If a child is still in nappies, they may need opportunities to touch themselves and masturbate. Linked to this, they will need provision of undisturbed time in a private space, such as their own bedroom. It may be appropriate to consider including time for touching themselves or masturbation on a child's private timetable to help them understand when and where this activity is appropriate. We need to remember that this activity is normal and can reduce stress and frustration. It will therefore impact on both general behaviour and confidence in learning toileting skills.

Preparing for adult life
Transition to Adult Services
The impact of continence difficulties can become more significant as children get older. It can have a major impact on opportunities for further education and study, employment and relationships.

Continence is an important area to consider when planning the young person's future accommodation and support needs, which may range from full-time specialist support through to independence. It is a time to consider any outstanding continence difficulties and is an excellent opportunity to review progress and plan and implement any new programmes needed.

Some teenagers respond well to the ideas of intensive training programmes. The idea of going to college or on an activity holiday, or becoming more independent, can be a powerful motivator to engage them in a toileting programme and be successful.

Intimate care
This may still be a need for some older children and will have to be addressed in planning and meeting their needs. It is helpful for both the young person and staff that their needs are included in a care plan which is reviewed by carers, family and the professionals involved. Even for young people with significant learning disabilities or limitations, it may be an opportunity to reconsider and attempt toilet training if needed. This will be of significant benefit for their dignity and security and can also reduce their care needs.

Provision of intimate care to young people who have physical or learning disabilities will need to ensure that their security, safety and dignity are protected. Local and national guidelines and policies will need to be adhered to.

Transfer of medical care

Paediatric services for many children may transfer to adult specialists if continued input is needed. The timing of this can vary dependent on a young person's needs or local resources, but usually happens when they leave school. It is essential to plan for this and ensure that there is a good handover of medical care. This includes information and discussion with the young person, and good communication and liaison with adult services. Many chronic conditions have excellent protocols in place which emphasise the need for planning, flexibility and information. One good example of this is for children with cystic fibrosis.[13]

For some young people, continuing medical care may be given and managed by their family doctor, who will also need up-to-date information about the young person's needs.

Care planning

Care plans are used to bring together a young person's health, social and educational needs. Toileting should be included in these where necessary in order to plan effectively for any additional support that is needed and to ensure that all individuals who are supporting the young person are providing this support consistently.

The use of multidisciplinary person-centred planning is a model of good practice when considering a young person's future needs. Planning for the future is complex and time-consuming and needs to be started as early as possible. There are different models of planning for transition to adult care, with the most important aspect being putting the young person's needs, wishes and abilities at the centre.

---

13 www.cysticfibrosis.org.uk/media/151254/FS%20-%20Transition%20-%20 commissioners_v2_Apr_2013.pdf

TOP TIPS

1. Work towards creating more independence regarding toileting and/or medication, but don't force it if the young person is not developmentally or emotionally ready.

2. Put toileting on the care plan and review regularly.

3. Discuss toileting as a key part of transition planning.

4. Review bowel and bladder function and medication.

5. Observe fluid intake and diet if this is something which needs addressing.

6. Observe where and when any problematic behaviour is occurring, and the triggers that may be involved.

Chapter 18

TOILET TEAMS THAT TALK TO EACH OTHER – THE ROAD TO SUCCESS!

Throughout this book, we have emphasised that one of the most essential factors for success in toilet training is to have an integrated team approach. This begins with preparation, and needs to continue throughout the process of supporting families and monitoring progress. It can build on success and effectively solve any problems that arise. The step-by-step approach described in the book should be used to review progress and work towards consolidation and development of further skills.

Building the toilet team can be challenging, and may involve different people for each child. The child and their parents are key members of the team. Children should be supported to participate in their toileting programme as much as they are able to.

Professionals need to remember that there can often be great difficulties for parents in participating fully in this process. It is helpful to consider the reasons for this, and essential not to assume that parents are not committed to engaging with toilet training. Apparent reluctance to engage may be linked to lack of support, previous failures, or being overwhelmed by the demands on the family. It may be necessary to consider carefully how to involve parents, and ensure that they are fully supported and treated as equal partners in planning and delivering care for their child.

Working as a team enables all members to develop their understanding and support and motivate each other. This is particularly important as many children with autism take a long time to learn to use the toilet and there are often many challenges along the way.

It is important to have access to a range of skills and perspectives from staff who know the child well. It is useful to include those involved with day care and out-of-school activities to ensure that toileting programmes are followed in all settings. This can help the child to learn the skills they need and enable them to learn flexibly and transfer these between settings.

Communication

Good communication is essential for the implementation of toileting programmes with consistency, and to promote consolidation of skills. Communication is not just about talking to each other; it includes ensuring that every team member is clearly informed about the details of the toilet training plan. These details need to be communicated clearly to everyone working with the child. This can be especially challenging when a child is being looked after in several care settings and it may be necessary to have a jointly agreed written plan.

The creation of a successful team that supports each other and communicates effectively requires promotion and facilitation by management teams. The implementation of policies and good practice guidelines is dependent on effective working at every level.

Why we should work collaboratively

Good joint working policies impact on the effectiveness of help for the child, especially in learning toileting skills. This is stated in *Every Child Matters* (Department for Education and Skills 2003):

> For children and young people there are five outcomes that are key to wellbeing in childhood and later life – being healthy, staying safe, enjoying and achieving, making a positive contribution and achieving economic wellbeing. These five constitute the focus of government attention for all pupils.

These recommendations focus on the importance of joint working to achieve the best outcomes for children. Difficulties in achieving successful joint working for children with autism and their families can be caused by the number and range of professionals and agencies involved in assessment, diagnosis, support, advice and therapy. As the child grows older, there may be many changes and variations in the team involved supporting the family. For some children there may be many professionals involved, whereas for others the support may be much less.

Implications of equality legislation

Equality legislation makes it clear that schools have to make reasonable adjustments and not put children with disabilities at substantial disadvantage. There is a legal requirement in the Equality Act 2010 to ensure that children are not discriminated against for a reason related to their disability. In practice this can mean not excluding children from attending school or participating in any associated activities because they are not reliably toilet trained.

The equality legislation informs national and local guidelines on ensuring a child's needs, and dignity is prioritised. Leaving a child in a soiled nappy or pants pending the return of a parent would be a substantial disadvantage and could be classed as a form of abuse (Carlin 2005). Reasonable adjustments related to toileting can also include the use of visual timetables and physical assistance with changing their nappies or cleaning themselves where necessary.

Failure to address a child's continence needs may create a more subtle difficulty for them to be accepted into their peer group and participate as fully in school activities as they are entitled to.

The advantages of effective joint working in toileting

- This is the most successful way of working, especially for children who have complex needs that affect several areas of their functioning.

- It is more likely to be effective in achieving successful toileting skills.

- It implements the skills and knowledge of people who know the child. It can often create a greater understanding of the child's needs and a holistic view of their situation.

- The child and parents have consistent messages and strategies used.

- Everyone gains a clearer understanding of the best way to support the child.

- It prevents confusion and conflicting information about toileting skills.

- Success in one area can create a ripple effect to help with implementing other strategies. Things that are successful in one place can be transferred to others.

- Professionals can gain insights and understanding of how to help the child in different settings.

- It may facilitate lateral thinking and inventive ideas about things that may work.

- It can relieve the need for families to explain the opinions of one professional to others.

- It can provide support for professionals and increase their skills and knowledge in the management of continence difficulties in children with autism.

- It ensures that for children with highly complex needs, any difficulties that may affect the success of a toileting programme will be considered and strategies will take account of these. This may include areas such as coordination difficulties, organisational problems and sensory differences.

Challenges that can prevent effective joint working

- Work load – often in many areas the work does not always seem to fit into the hours available. It can be a challenge to arrange meetings at a time that everyone can manage to fit in with other work commitments.

- There is a need to keep good notes of meetings and decisions. Someone has to do this.

- Different agendas – professionals may have different outcomes and aims for the children they are working with. It can be a challenge to develop a dialogue with staff from other agencies and disciplines.

- Different priorities – each setting may prioritise different needs; there may be a need to negotiate and agree the different priorities between professional groups.

- There may be a need to provide training for some people working with children with autism – to build their confidence, skills, knowledge and understanding to enable them to provide appropriate support.

- Variable environments – it may be difficult to implement strategies in different settings linked to organisational variations in staffing and skills.

- Management constraints – managers may not perceive the need for joint working, or create an environment where this is facilitated.

- Children are not the same in different settings – there may be a number of distractions or other demands upon them, making learning toileting more difficult in some settings.

- Children change all the time, especially as they get older.

- Each day varies for children and professionals. Children are sometimes tired or cross, and may not respond consistently. Professionals also get tired or stressed at times.

- Staff changes.

- Services for families may vary at different times in the child's life, and different professionals may be involved. They need to get to know the child, and may have other ideas, which may differ from those agreed previously.

- Often services are reorganised and changed and this can disrupt the consistent development of team approaches.

An example of the effects of different priorities for children with bowel and bladder problems sometimes arises in school linked to healthy eating policies. The suggestion of offering rewards of crisps or sweets for using the toilet may appear to be in direct conflict with a school's healthy eating policy.

The use of food rewards would need to be discussed and agreed to prevent the child having different rewards at school and at home. While we would all subscribe to the importance of healthy eating, it is also important to help children become toilet trained and how to do this will need to be negotiated.

How do we make it happen?

However useful joint working may be, it will not happen unless someone thinks about it, plans it and arranges it. There is a need to make the first contacts, negotiate appropriate timing and venue, and make sure it is convenient for everyone.

It is essential to involve parents and carers. You may need to acknowledge that it can be difficult at times for parents to attend meetings due to many factors such as work commitments, other children, elderly parents, other professionals to see, or transport or travel problems.

It is equally essential to involve the child, in a way that is appropriate for the individual themselves, taking into account their understanding, abilities and motivation. The child's perspective can be very valuable. This could be sought through asking them or observed from their behaviour. Children can sometimes express their views using drawing, puppets or play activities.

There is a need to establish who should be included, usually after discussion with the family. It is important to have all the people with relevant information and skills (though it is not always necessary to include everyone). Although there may be regular care planning meetings taking place, it is sometimes necessary to get relevant people together to just focus on the toileting plans.

The overall needs of the child should be clarified and this should include an understanding of their strengths and interests.

There should be clear objectives and priorities agreed for the process, timing, and review of progress. There should be a detailed agreed plan of action that is achievable and does not put stress on any one individual or service.

Schools and parents should be helped to appreciate that although successful toileting may take time and effort, it will create significantly more time to do and learn other things, and should be seen as an education and social benefit.

Models of joint working

These will vary depending on how services are organised and delivered. Different areas and countries often have different structures and resources for working with children with autism. There are many ways of achieving this, and some will be more appropriate at different settings and times.

A key group of professionals can be created to deal with specific issues. This group may vary for different aspects of a child's needs.

Within one setting or organisation there may be one professional who has a role to liaise with others and feed back to their colleagues, for example the school nurse or specialist teacher.

A particular way of approaching this is the Key Working[14] model, in which a key worker takes the lead in facilitation of joint working strategies. The key worker may be appointed with a specific role to coordinate services for the child. This model has been utilised in many areas and can be very valuable for families. Not all families have allocated key workers, and the role may be taken on by one of the professionals working with the child. This may be included as part of their professional responsibilities, but to be effective there needs to be adequate time allocated.

Sometimes a family member may want to take on a lead coordination role, and this may help them to feel in control. However, it is essential that they have the skills, willingness, time and resources to do this as it can be demanding and stressful.

Some organisations may arrange for specific training and advice to develop their skills and expertise. Development of a skilled team

---

14 www.councilfordisabledchildren.org.uk/news/january-june-2014/new-developing-key-working-guide

in an organisation may be very valuable, and can help to support others working with the child, and also other children. Input and advice from specialised services could be a key part of this.

What toileting guidelines should include

It is always helpful to have clear guidelines available to ensure good communication and clarity of the child's needs (see the Sample Toileting Management Plan in the Practical Tools section). This ensures consistency, and is especially important when there may be different carers involved. The guidelines should include:

- Child's name, age, family names and structure and family contact details.

- Contact names and details of professionals involved with the child, especially the name of a key worker if there is one.

- Clarification of diagnosis, bowel and bladder problems, and outlook for the future.

- Agreed toileting targets, strategies and rewards.

- Clarification of language, signs or objects of reference to be used.

- Details of daily routines.

- Advice about diet and fluids, including any reasonable adjustments for the welfare of the child that consider individual patterns and any rigidity that may affect eating and drinking.

- Information and advice about medication, its effectiveness and side-effects.

- Information about continence products and their disposal.

- Advice about cleaning and changing the child if needed).

- The impact of continence upon a child's ability to achieve other targets in social skills and learning.

- Advice about trips out to other venues and, if needed, overnight stays.

- Strategies to develop strengths, skills and enthusiasms.

- Information about possible future investigations and treatment if needed.

- Relevant information about the child's medical problems.

- Details of support resources and groups.

Some important transition times for discussion of toileting problems

Diagnosis

The timing of this varies, and may be affected by the severity of the child's condition, the concerns of the family and others who know the child, and identification of the child's problems. It frequently includes a number of different professionals from health, education, psychology and children's services. It is invariably a stressful time for parents and carers and it is often difficult for them to absorb the implications of a diagnosis and all the information given.

It is an excellent time to identify which professionals may be needed to deal with specific problems including toileting, and make a plan for future management and input. It may not be the time to make detailed recommendations about toileting, but the professionals involved and the process for planning and support can be clearly agreed. Written information for families and professionals is essential as well as follow-up input, support and information about other helpful resources.

Starting school

This is an important time in any child's life, and is especially difficult for children with autism. It is a key time to discuss any toileting needs and to ensure that the staff at school understand and manage these needs appropriately. As children are starting school, there is an expectation that they will be toilet trained, and it is essential to ensure that education colleagues understand the difficulties the child has and how these link to their autism.

It can be an excellent opportunity to help the child realise the importance and benefits of using the toilet. In a new situation it can be possible to make changes to a child's toileting routine, although it is not always easy or appropriate for all children. The importance of being continent makes a significant impact on a child's ability to integrate socially and fit into an educational setting.

There can be considerable challenges to management in school, including ensuring that staff are in place to meet a child's agreed toileting needs and provide support. It is a great asset for the staff to have information, support and advice from professionals with expertise in toileting, and have an agreed plan in place. It is an opportunity to create a joint understanding about the aim to achieve continence, and the steps needed to be in place to achievethis.

It is often necessary to consider resources needed for a child, including which toilet would be most appropriate for them to use, considering their social needs, understanding, and specific motor and sensory differences. There may be a requirement for help with changing and cleaning children, and this will have staffing implications. The resources needed may also have financial implications for the school. It is essential that schools identify staff with the time available and the skills to support children with continence needs.

Many children with autism will have additional educational needs and some may require special provision. Children with autism who attend mainstream schools may also have significant toileting difficulties, and schools will vary in their experience and resources for dealing with these. At times, school staff may have difficulty in understanding why children who are accepted into a mainstream setting have significant needs in developing toileting skills. These difficulties are rarely linked to parents not attempting toilet training – they have usually tried extremely hard with this.

School reviews

Educational plans for children with special needs are reviewed regularly. It is helpful to include targets on learning toileting skills. In this way, toileting is given equal importance with other learning targets. Where children have bowel and bladder problems, especially constipation, these are likely to impact upon their learning, concentration and social skills.

Transferring school

The toileting needs of children need to be communicated when children transfer school, and it is an excellent opportunity to review progress, build on success and share strategies. Changing schools can be stressful for children, and preparation and continued support will be necessary. Routines and rewards also need to be reviewed and may need to be made age-appropriate.

It is a good opportunity to review a child's needs and, if appropriate, reassess their bowel and bladder function and the impact of their autism and learning difficulties on their toileting.

It should never be assumed that it is too late to start toilet training for any child with autism.

There is often a need to review resources and toileting facilities in schools for older children, including privacy, changing needs and protection from bullying. As children are becoming older, it is also a good opportunity to discuss with others who know the child the possibilities of their taking on increasing responsibility for their personal needs, appropriate to their level of abilities.

Tom was eight years old and had a review of his education plan with the school staff, his parents and his paediatrician. He was attending a mainstream school and making good progress with his learning. There were some concerns about his behaviour – he was getting angry and throwing things. It was noticed that this happened mostly on Thursdays when he and his class had a supply teacher and they did art.

Tom's parents pointed out that he was also constipated and withholding and this became worse as the week went by. The doctor suggested it might help to increase his constipation medication on Tuesdays and also Wednesdays if needed.

His teacher agreed to ask him to go to his special toilet after lunch on Wednesdays and Thursdays. The change in routine helped to achieve a more regular bowel pattern, and his teacher noticed that he was also less irritable and engaged better with his art projects. They agreed that his project could focus on machine parts – which was what he liked to play with.

Child protection or safeguarding concerns

It is important that we do not automatically see the presentation of toileting difficulties as an indicator of abuse. At the same time, it is crucial that children are protected and there is a prompt response to any concerns of possible neglect or abuse.

Where there is any concern about the quality of a child's care there is a need for multidisciplinary discussion and assessment.

Children with autism often create many challenges for families, and occasionally give rise to child protection concerns. Continence problems are particularly challenging and stressful for families to manage, and these difficulties may at times affect the quality of a child's care.

Continence difficulties in children, especially soiling, at times may give rise to concern about possible abuse. It can be a way for the child to communicate. It is vitally important to fully evaluate the child's whole situation to try to determine if the continence problems are linked to other factors.

Sometimes families may find it difficult to cope with toileting problems together with the other demands on them. It may be difficult for them to initiate a discussion about wetting and soiling, because they are fearful of being judged as inadequate parents. The stress and anxiety in families may aggravate toileting problems further and set up a deteriorating cycle, affecting the way a child is cared for. Where this occurs, there is a need for professionals to meet and liaise to assess the problems fully and support the child and the parents. The child's welfare and safety will be paramount in deciding the best course of action.

Chapter 19

FINALLY, MOVING ON

In the last thirty years the knowledge and understanding of autism and its variability has developed and changed, and has become widely accepted. It seems inevitable that this will continue in the future and the outlook for people with autism will continue to expand and develop.

Children are all different. Many of them learn how to use the toilet, and move on and never need to think of their toilet training again. For others there may be a need for consolidation and reminders, sometimes for a considerable time. While it is the final objective to enable the child or young person to be as independent as possible, we all need to ensure that they have the support and help they need for as long as necessary.

People with special needs can be vulnerable at times. We need to remember that, especially for people who have continence needs, they may be more dependent on others and there is a potential risk of abuse. However difficult they may be to learn, the acquisition of continence skills gives a person dignity, and increases their personal safety and security.

Why should we persevere?

It is important to emphasise the range of opportunities that become available and easier when there is no need to consider continence issues.

For younger children, this includes friendships, opportunity to visit friends and extended family, as well as sleepovers, camping and school trips. It is a new world when there is no need to remember to take spare clothes! For some children the improvement may be felt by having more time for things they love, such as time on the computer, or playing games. It is particularly important for children with autism to have time for activities that help them build their social skills and understanding.

Older children who are reliably clean and dry will have increased opportunities for travel, employment, further education and independent living. There may be a significant impact upon personal and social interaction, including self-esteem, love, sexual needs and long-term relationships and partners.

As professionals and caregivers we have an ethical responsibility and duty to address continence. There are many children and adults with autism who have not received effective toilet training, usually because it is felt they cannot be trained. There is now information available and a significant range of resources and effective strategies that can be used to achieve this. Advice and training may be extremely valuable, and are available from professionals with expertise and skills in continence management.

Rights

The Human Rights Act 1998, based on the European Convention on Human Rights, includes the following criteria:

- Right to liberty and security

- Respect for your private and family life, home and correspondence

- Right to marry and start a family

- Protection from discrimination in respect of these rights and freedoms

- Right to education.

This suggests that the provision of help towards continence is a right for people with autism, and not an option. However difficult it may be for carers and professionals to implement, this help and support is essential to ensure the dignity, welfare and independence of a person with autism.

At times it may be the easier option to continue using continence protection, especially when there are other significant needs. We would argue that this is an option that may be sometimes for the benefit of the carers, and the rights of the individual with autism must take priority to be evaluated, met and respected.

On 20 May 2014, the European Court of Human Rights ruled that the failure of local authorities to consider a person's dignity can lead to a breach of their human rights under Article 8, Respect for the Right to a Private Life.

Sue Bott, Director of Policy and Development, Disability Rights UK, commented:[15]

> 'We are encouraged that the ECHR has taken the view that dignity and respect for a private life should be taken into account when the State is taking decisions regarding support to disabled people. This sends out a helpful message to those challenging their care plans. Local authorities must now balance decisions to make savings with the need to positively uphold an individual's right to dignity, a private life and independence.'

This supports a view that care plans should respect a person's human rights and dignity, and creates a framework upon which meeting a person's continence needs can be based.

Celebrating progress and success

Reaching your goal is a wonderful feeling for all involved. However much time, effort and struggle it takes, it will always be worth it. One thing to remember is that there will be more time for other things, along with significant financial savings in continence products, washing powder, energy and clothing.

---

15   www.disabilityrightsuk.org

The goal for some children may be an intermediate target, and it is important for all concerned to celebrate each success along the way. There may be a need for everyone to have a break before the next stage; a pause in training may be an opportunity to consolidate the skills acquired. It is helpful to make a plan to return to the task and this ensures that toilet training does not get lost in the many other demands that life presents.

There are numerous problems that children and adults with autism have to deal with throughout their life. Addressing continence is vital to increase independence and self-esteem, and creates more time, opportunity and energy to deal with other challenges and develop other learning and skills.

The future of autism and continence

We do not yet fully understand the reasons why some children with autism become toilet trained at a similar age to other children, and why others have difficulties. We really do not know exactly why some children are successful. There needs to be more dialogue about problems of continence, including views from people with autism. It would help others to learn what they found helpful, and unhelpful. A wider discussion would help with understanding, leading to addressing the problem more effectively. We are sure that good stories about toileting skills, written for children by people with autism, would be a brilliant resource.

Becoming continent is a much more important skill than reading and writing, so why aren't there any good computer games to help to teach toilet training skills? We hope someone in the technical world is working on a body sensor connected to a mobile phone that buzzes when the bladder is full.

Why has no one written a good computer programme that parents can insert into computer games that flashes up after a set time: 'This game cannot continue until the player has been to the toilet and done a wee'?! Maybe success with going to the toilet could be linked to a bonus score.

How great would it be if someone could develop a seat sensor that activates a signal when the child's bladder is full, and they start to wriggle!

And finally, our last word goes to a parent

'We very rarely remember our toileting difficulties now, as we are busy dealing with the teenage years: a whole new set of challenges! Our son is now a great tall 15-year-old, who copes with life amazingly, and of whom we are really proud.' *(Jacqui Eames)*

PRACTICAL TOOLS

BOWEL AND BLADDER RECORDING CHART

	Day 1	Day 2	Day 3	Day 4	Day 5	Day 6	Day 7
Date							
Time	Wet Dry Soiled	Wet Dry Soiled	Wet Dry Soiled	Wet Dry Soiled	Wet Dry Soiled	Wet Dry Soiled	Wet Dry Soiled
7.00 7.30							
8.00 8.30							
9.00 9.30							
10.00 10.30							

★

11.00
11.30

12.00
12.30

1.00
1.30

2.00
2.30

3.00
3.30

4.00
4.40

5.00
5.30

6.00
6.30

7.00
7.30

8.00
8.30

★

TOILET READINESS ASSESSMENT

	Always	Often	Occasionally	Never
Understanding				
Understands visual cues and/or objects of reference				
Verbal language				
Response to commands				
Motor skills				
Reliable balance				
Accurate fine motor ability				

Awareness

Indicates bowel or bladder activity

Empties bowel or bladder in a selected place

Shows interest in others using the toilet

Bladder maturity

Able to hold wee for 1–2 hours

Dry during daytime naps

Dry nappies at night

Bowel functioning

Regular bowel pattern

Presence of constipation

Presence of diarrhoea or loose bowels

★

BEHAVIOURAL ASSESSMENT

Behaviours	Present	Intermittent	Absent
Anxiety			
Rigid behaviour			
Sensory difficulties			
Routines and rituals			
Ability to transfer skills to other situations			
Ability to understand sequences of activities			
Good understanding of words or symbols			
Behaviour – anger and meltdowns			
Behaviour – withdrawal			

★

PROGRESS RECORDING AND MONITORING CHART

	Clean and dry	Wee in the toilet	Poo in the toilet	Wet s/m/l*	Soiled s/m/l*	Medicine
Monday am pm						
Tuesday am pm						
Wednesday am pm						
Thursday am pm						

★

	Clean and dry	Wee in the toilet	Poo in the toilet	Wet s/m/l*	Soiled s/m/l*	Medicine
Friday am						
pm						
Saturday am						
pm						
Sunday am						
pm						

Note: s/m/l – small/medium/large

★

Charlie's Story

My name is Charlie and I am 8 and live with my Daddy and our dog Albert.

I go to school, and I like PE. I like playing with my friend Isabel. I like running, hopscotch and dancing.

I am learning how our body works. We eat food to make us grow and have energy. What we don't need comes out of our bottom as poo.

People learn to let go their poos in the toilet, as this is smart. After they do a poo people wipe their bottom with soft toilet paper, just enough to get their bottoms clean. They often need to do a poo every day and afterwards they flush the toilet so it is kept clean. The poo goes down the toilet to the sewage works where it is made nice. Using the toilet is clever and it keeps our pants clean. After they use the toilet, people wash their hands so any germs are washed off.

I can get myself dressed now.

I am trying to learn to wipe my bottom after I have finished doing my poo. I take one wet wipe and carefully clean my bottom from front to back. I will then use another piece and if it is clean, I can pull up my pants.

If there is a lot of poo, I can ask a grown-up to help me.

Ronnie's Story

My name is Ronnie and I like spacemen and fish. I am five and I live with my Mummy and Daddy, and my brothers Tim and Johnny. I walk to school with my brother Tim and my Mummy. I am in Mrs Smith's class, she is very nice. I like choosing toys to play with in the quiet corner.

I am growing up, and I can get myself dressed, and put my own socks on. I can count to five. I am learning to use the toilet. At school I use the school toilet. Most children use school toilets if they need to wee, children at school can do this. Mrs Smith will tell me at break it is toilet time. It is good to use the toilet before going out to play.

Sometimes I do my poo after breakfast in the toilet at home. If I need to do a poo at school I can go to the toilet at school and Mrs Smith will help me.

My Mummy and Daddy are pleased when I do a poo in the toilet. When I do this I can play with my spaceship game.

KEIRA'S TOP TOILETING TIPS

	Marks out of 10 ✓
Race my poo to the toilet	
Sit on the toilet until all the poo has come out	
Get toilet paper and wipe my bottom	
If some poo leaks out I should go as soon as I can to clean myself	
I should put dirty pants in a bucket	
I can ask for help if I cannot get myself clean	
Wash my hands	

ENVIRONMENTAL SENSORY AUDIT

For each item mentioned, consider whether this is something the child is hyper- or hyposensitive to; is it something they are seeking input from or wanting to actively avoid?

Sensory system	Potential areas of difficulty	Potential adaptations
Tactile (touch)	Toilet seat Toilet rolls or wipes Nappy Splashes from the toilet Need to fiddle when sitting on the toilet Temperature Touching poo	
Vestibular (balance)	Toilet seat Flooring Reflections	
Proprioception (body awareness)	Toilet seat Body positioning Nappy or pants Clothing Labels in clothes Awareness of need to wee or poo Navigating around bathroom	
Visual (sight)	Walls Lighting Brightness Bathroom fitments Mirrors Items in line of sight	
Auditory (hearing)	Toilet flush Splashing in toilet Sounds from pipes, fans, hand-dryers Echoes	

Sensory system	Potential areas of difficulty	Potential adaptations
Olfactory (smell)	Wee and poo Bathroom products (cleaning and toiletries) Air-fresheners	
Gustatory (taste)	Bathroom products (cleaning and toiletries) Air-fresheners Poo	

SAMPLE TOILETING MANAGEMENT PLAN

RE: JC
Age: 8 years
Family: Parents, sisters aged 5 and 3 years
School: Special school for learning difficulties
Consultant:
Other professionals:
GP:
Problems: Developmental delay
Autism
Immaturity in learning toileting skills
Bladder urgency and constipation
Overflow soiling at night
Skills: JC is friendly and likes to please his teachers
He likes Dippy the dinosaur and going on the trampoline

Treatment Plan

- Include toileting targets as a part of his overall support and learning plan.

- Words for wee, poo and toilet to be agreed with parents.

- Encourage regular toilet visits at agreed times in the school day – with reminders on his timetable and a picture cue of his toilet.

- J is to be taken to the toilet, pull his trousers and pants down, and sit on it for a timed amount, up to 3 minutes.

- Encourage J to sit on the toilet – he needs a hand-rail to feel secure.

- Ensure a good fluid intake of clear watery fluids, 7 drinks a day – he likes pink drinks.

- Encourage fibre as part of healthy eating.

- Give praise and rewards for practising using the toilet – he likes a dinosaur dot-to-dot.

- Encourage him to try different toilets at school and when visiting relatives.

- Provide regular feedback of progress and discussion with parents about modification of targets.

- Ensure a regular bowel pattern using Movicol medication and maintaining and adjusting this as needed (information is attached for school and also given to parents).

- Record the bowel pattern and toilet success on the charts, at school and at home.

- Review progress at the beginning of next term.

Further advice is available from the specialist school nurse and paediatrician about his medication. Information about bowel and bladder training is available from ERIC (www.eric.org.uk) and PromoCon.

BIBLIOGRAPHY

Ayres, A.J. (2005) *Sensory Integration and the Child.* Los Angeles, CA: Western Psychological Services.

Baron-Cohen, S. (2008) *Autism and Asperger Syndrome (The Facts).* Oxford: Oxford University Press.

Black, T. (n.d.) *Poo Go Home.* Available at www.eric.org.uk/Shop/product/34, accessed on 15 April 2015.

Bondy, A., and Frost, L. (1994) 'The Picture Exchange Communication system.' *Focus on Autistic Behaviour 9,* 3, 1–19.

Bromley, D. (2014) 'Abdominal massage in the management of chronic constipation for children with disability.' *Community Practitioner 87,* 12, 25–29.

Butler, R.J., and Heron, J. (2008) 'The prevalence of infrequent bedwetting and nocturnal enuresis in childhood.' *Scandinavian Journal of Urology and Nephrology 42,* 257–264.

Butler, R.J., and McKenna, S. (2002) 'Overcoming parental intolerance in childhood nocturnal enuresis.' *BJU International 89,* 3, 295–297.

Cameron, K., and Tebbi, M.D. (1993) 'Treatment compliance in childhood and adolescence.' *Cancer 71,* Issue Supplement S10, 3441–3449.

Carlin, J. (2005) *Including Me – Managing Complex Health Needs in Schools and Early Years Settings.* London: Council for Disabled Children. Available at www.westsussex.gov.uk/idoc.ashx?docid=bd9e675d-7c1c-4369-8722-dbb2b3aca35a&version=-1, accessed on 17 April 2015.

Christie, P., Duncan, M., Fidler, R., and Healy, Z. (2011) *Understanding Pathological Demand Avoidance Syndrome in Children: A Guide for Parents, Teachers and Other Professionals.* London: Jessica Kingsley Publishers.

Clements, J. (2005) *People With Autism Behaving Badly.* London: Jessica Kingsley Publishers.

Cohn, A. (2007) *Constipation, Withholding and Your Child: A Family Guide to Soiling and Wetting.* London: Jessica Kingsley Publishers.

Coucouvanis, J.A. (2008) *The Potty Journey.* Shawnee Mission, KS: Autism Asperger Publishing Company.

Cystic Fibrosis Trust (2013) *Transition from Paediatric to Adult Care: A Guide for Commissioners, Hospital and Clinical teams.* Available at www.cysticfibrosis. org.uk/media/151254/FS%20-%20Transition%20-%20commissioners_ v2_Apr_2013.pdf, accessed on 17 April 2015.

Department for Education and Skills (2003) *Every Child Matters.* London: HMSO.

Duel, B.P., Steinberg-Epstein, R., Hill, M., and Lerner, M. (2003) 'A survey of voiding dysfunction in children with attention deficit-hyperactivity disorder.' *The Journal of Urology. 170,* 4 part 2, 1521–1523; Discussion, 2523–2524.

Ertan, P., Yilmaz,O., Caglayan, M., Sogut, A., Aslan, S., and Yuksel, H. (2009) 'Relationship of sleep quality of life in children with monosymptomatic enuresis.' *Child: Care, Health and Development 35,* 4, 469–474.

Franklin, S., with Sanderson, H. (2014) *Personalisation in Practice, Supporting Young People with Disabilities through the Transition to Adulthood.* London: Jessica Kingsley Publishers.

Godfrey, M. (2014) Tate Modern Exhibition Guide.

Gray, C. (2010) *The New Social Story Book.* Arlington, TX: Future Horizons.

Handel, L.N., Barqawi, A., Checa, G., Furness, P.D., and Koyle, M.A. (2003) 'Males with Down's syndrome and non-neurogenic bladder.' *The Journal of Urology 169,* 2, 646–649.

Hannah, L. (2001) *Teaching Young Children With Autism Spectrum Disorders to Learn: A Practical Guide for Parents and Staff in Mainstream Schools and Nurseries.* London: The National Autistic Society.

Hicks, J.A., Carson, C., and Malone, P.S. (2007) 'Is there an association between functional bladder outlet obstruction and Down's syndrome?' *Journal of Pediatric Urology. 3,*5, 369–374.

Howlin, P., and Asgharian, A. (1999) 'The diagnosis of autism and Asperger syndrome: findings from a survey of 770 families.' *Developmental Medicine and Child Neurology 41,* 834–839.

Huang, T., Shu, X., Huang, Y.S., and Cheuk, D.K.L. (2011) *Complementary Treatments such as Hypnosis, Psychotherapy, Acupuncture, Chiropractic and Medicinal Herbs for Bedwetting in Children.* London: Cochrane Incontinence Group. Available at http://summaries.cochrane.org/CD005230/INCONT_ complementary-treatments-such-as-hypnosis-psychotherapy-acupuncture-chiropractic-and-medicinal-herbs-for-bedwetting-in-children, accessed on 17 April 2015.

Joint Formulary Committee (2015) *British National Formulary 69.* London: BMJ Publishing Group and Royal Pharmaceutical Society. Available at www.pharmpress.com/product/9780857111562/bnf69, accessed on 15 April 2015.

Jolliffe, T., Landsdown, R., and Robinson, T. (1992) *Autism: A Personal Account.* London: The National Autism Society.

Kenney, W.L., and Chiu, P. (2001) 'Influence on age of thirst and fluid intake.' *Medicine and Science in Sport and Exercise 33*,1524–1532.

Klintwall, L., Holm, A., Eriksson, M., Carlsson, L.H., *et al.* (2010) 'Sensory abnormalities in autism.' *Research in Developmental Disabilities 32*, 795–800.

Ktuscher, M.L., and Attwood, A. (2014) *Kids in the Syndrome Mix of ADHD, LD, Autism Spectrum Disorder, Tourette's, Anxiety and More!* London: Jessica Kingsley Publishers.

Kupferman, J.C., Druschel, C.M., and Kupchik, G.S. (2009) 'Increased prevalence of renal and urinary tract abnormalities in children with Down's syndrome.' *Paediatrics 124*, 4, 615–621.

Laurie, C. (2013) *Sensory Strategies: Practical Ways to Help Children and Young People With Autism Learn and Achieve.* London: The National Autistic Society.

Lukacz, E.S., Sampselle, C., Gray, M., MacDiarmid, S., Rosenberg, M., Ellsworth, P., and Palmer, M.H. (2011) 'A healthy bladder. A consensus statement.' *International Journal of Clinical Practice 65*, 10,1026–1036.

Mackner, L.M., and Crandall, W.V. (2005) 'Oral medication adherence in pediatric inflammatory bowel disease.' *Inflamm. Bowel Dis. 11*, 1006–1012.

McClurg, D., and Lowe-Strong, A. (2011) 'Does abdominal massage relieve constipation?' *Nursing Times 107*, 12, 20–22.

Mengoni, S., Oates, J., and Bardsley, J. (2014) *Developing Key Working.* Milton Keynes: The Open University. Available at www.councilfordisabledchildren. org.uk/news/january-june-2014/new-developing-key-working-guide.

Mesibov, G.B., Shea, V., and Schopler, E. (2004) *The TEACCH Approach to Autism Spectrum Disorders.* London: Springer.

Meydan, E.A., Civilibal, M., Elevli, M., Duru, N.S., and Civilibal, N. (2012) 'The quality of life of mothers of children with monosymptomatic enuresis nocturna.' *International Urology and Nephrology 44*, 3, 655–659.

National Collaborating Centre for Women's and Children's Health (2007) *Urinary Tract Infection in Children: Diagnosis, Treatment and Long-Term Management.* London. National Institute for Clinical Excellence.

National Institute for Clinical Excellence (2012) *Nocturnal Enuresis: The Management of Bedwetting in Children and Young People.* Clinical Guideline 111. Available at www.nice.org.uk/guidance/CG111, accessed on 17 April 2015.

National Institute for Health and Clinical Excellence (2007) *Urinary Tract Infection in Children: Diagnosis, Treatment and Long-Term Management.* Clinical Guideline 54. Available at www.nice.org.uk/guidance/CG54, accessed on 17 April 2015.

National Institute for Health and Clinical Excellence (NICE) (2010) *Constipation in Children and Young People.* Clinical Guideline 99. Available at www.nice. org.uk/guidance/CG99, accessed on 17 April 2015.

Nevéus, T., Hetta, J., Cnattingius, S., Tuvemo, T., *et al.* (1999) 'Depth of sleep and sleep habits among enuretic and incontinent children.' *Acta Paediatrica* 88, 7, 748–752.

Nevéus, T., von Gontard, A., Hoebeke, P., Hjälmås, K., *et al.* (2006) 'The standardization of terminology of lower urinary tract function in children and adolescents: report from the standardisation committee of the international children's continence society.' *Journal of Urology 176*, 314–324.

Nevins, T.E. (2002) 'Non-compliance and its management in teenagers.' *Pediatric Transplantation 6*, 475–479.

Newson, E., in collaboration with Christie, P., and staff of Sutherland House School (1998) *Education and Handling Guidelines for Children with Pathological Demand Avoidance Syndrome.* Nottingham: Information Service, Elizabeth Newson Centre, Ravenshead, Nottingham.

Paediatric Continence Forum (2014) *Commissioning Guide for Paediatric Continence.* Available at www.paediatriccontinenceforum.org, accessed on 17 April 2015.

PDA Society (2014) *Pathological Demand Avoidance Syndrome: A Reference Booklet for Clinicians.* Available at www.pdasociety.org.uk/resources/awareness-matters-booklet, accessed on 17 April 2015.

Powell, A. (2011) *Autism: Understanding and Managing Anger.* London: The National Autistic Society.

Reynolds, K. (2014a) *Tom Needs to Go.* London: Jessica Kingsley Publishers.

Reynolds, K. (2014b) *Sexuality and Severe Autism: A Practical Guide for Parents, Caregivers and Health Educators.* London: Jessica Kingsley Publishers.

Rittig, S., Schaumburg, H.L., Siggaard, C., Schmidt, F., and Djurhuus, J.C. (2008) 'The circadian defect in plasma vasopressin and urine output is related to desmopressin response and enuresis status in children with nocturnal enuresis.' *The Journal of Urology 179*, 6, 2389–2395.

Rogers, J., and Patricolo, M. (2014) *Understanding Bladder & Bowel Comorbidities in Children & Young People With Additional Needs – The Importance of Assessment.* PromoCon. Available at www.disabledliving.co.uk/DISLIV/media/publicationpdf/The%20Platinum%20Trust%20Resources/17549-bladder---bowel.pdf, accessed on 17 April 2015.

Roijen, L.E.G., Postema, K., Limbeek, V.J., and Kuppevelt, V.H.J.M. (2001) 'Development of bladder control in children and adolescents with cerebral palsy.' *Developmental Medicine and Child Neurology 43*,103–107.

Royal College of Nursing (2006) *Paediatric Assessment of Toilet Training Readiness and The Issuing of Products.* An RCN Pathway. London: RCN.

Sinclair, M. (2011) 'The use of abdominal massage to treat chronic constipation.' *Journal of Bodywork and Movement Therapies 15*, 4, 436–445. Available at www.ncbi.nlm.nih.gov/pubmed/21943617, accessed on 17 April 2015.

Singer, S. (n.d.) *Eat a Rainbow Every Day.* Available at www.eatarainboweveryday.com, accessed on 17 April 2015.

Smith-Myles, B. (2001) *Asperger Syndrome and Sensory Issues: Practical Solutions for Making Sense of the World.* Shawnee Mission, KS: Autism Asperger Publishing Company.

UK Government (2004) *Children Act.* London: HMSO.

Van den Berg, M.M., Benninga, M.A., and Di Lorenzo, C. (2006) 'Epidemiology of childhood constipation: a systematic review.' *The American Journal of Gastroenterology 101,* 10, 2401–2409.

Van Laecke, E., Golinveaux, L., Goossens, L., Raes, A., *et al.* (2001) 'Voiding disorders in severely mentally and motor disabled children.' *The Journal of Urology. 166,* 6, 2404–2406.

Vande Walle, J., Rittig, S., Bauer, S., Eggert, P., *et al.* (2012) 'Practical consensus guidelines for the management of enuresis.' *European Journal of Paediatrics 171,* 971–983.

Von Gontard, A. (2012) 'Does psychological stress affect lower urinary tract function in children?' *Neurourology and Urodynamics 31,* 3, 3444–3448.

Wheeler, M. (1998) *Toilet Training for Individuals with Autism and Related Disorders.* Arlington, TX: Future Horizons.

Whitaker, P. (2001) *Challenging Behaviour and Autism.* London: The National Autistic Society.

Williams, I., and Wright, Y. (n.d.) *Sneaky Poo.* Available at www.eric.org.uk, accessed on 17 April 2015.

Wing, L., and Gould, J. (1979). 'Severe impairments of social interaction and associated abnormalities in children: epidemiology and classification.' *Journal of Autism & Developmental Disorders 9,* 11–29.

Woodcock, L., and Page, A. (2010) *Managing Family Meltdown: The Low Arousal Approach and Autism.* London: Jessica Kingsley Publishers.

Wrobel, M. (2003) *Taking Care Of Myself: A Healthy Hygiene, Puberty and Personal Curriculum For Young People With Autism.* Arlington, TX: Future Horizons.

Yack, E., Sutton, S., and Aquilla, P. (2002) *Building Bridges Through Sensory Integration: Therapy for Children with Autism and Other Pervasive Development Disorders.* Las Vegas, NV: Sensory Resources.

Yeung, C.K., Sihoe, J.D.Y., Sit, F.K.Y., Bower, W., Sreedhar, B., and Lau, J. (2004) 'Characteristics of primary nocturnal enuresis in adults: an epidemiological study.' *BJU International 93,* 3, 341–345.

RESOURCES

Listed below are a variety of organisations, books or resources that may be useful for helping with toileting difficulties. Many of these have been suggested by the families and practitioners that we have both met over the years!

UK Organisations
ERIC
The UK's leading childhood continence charity. They provide information and support on childhood bedwetting, daytime wetting, constipation and soiling to children, young people, parents and professionals. They offer a confidential helpline and have an online shop where you can buy a wide array of continence products, including bed protection. They provide training for professionals in the management of childhood bladder and bowel difficulties.

www.eric.org.uk
0845 370 8008 (open Monday and Wednesday, 9.30–4.30)

PromoCon
They provide a national service, working as part of Disabled Living, Manchester, to improve the life for all people with bladder or bowel problems. They offer a confidential helpline, product information,

advice and practical solutions to professionals and the general public.

www.promocon.co.uk
0161 834 2001 (open Monday to Friday, 9.00–4.00)

Toilet training

www.disabledliving.co.uk/Promocon/Publications/Children/
Toilet-Training

Bedwetting and bladder problems

www.disabledliving.co.uk/Promocon/Publications/Children/
Bladder
Constipation and bowel problems
www.disabledliving.co.uk/Promocon/Publications/Children/
Bowels

The National Autistic Society

The leading UK charity for people with autism (including Asperger syndrome) and their families. They provide information, support and pioneering services, and campaign for a better world for people with autism.

www.autism.org.uk
0808 800 4104 (open Monday to Friday, 10.00–4.00)

Free resources and UK guidance
One Step at a Time

This information booklet and set of tip sheets is for parents of a child with special needs. It guides parents through the process of developing toileting skills and toilet training, and resources include illustrations to help children understand the steps to learn to use the toilet. It also has an accompanying app.

www.continencevictoria.org.au/resources/one-step-time-parents-
guide-toilet-skills-children-special-needs

Visual Aids for Learning
Website for visual symbols and routines.

www.visualaidsforlearning.com

Do2Learn
Website for visual symbols and routines.

www.do2learn.com

Guidelines
NICE: *Guidelines on Constipation in Children and Young People*
http://guidance.nice.org.uk/CG99/NICEGuidance/pdf/English

NICE: *Guidelines on Nocturnal Enuresis: The Management of Bedwetting in Children and Young People*
http://guidance.nice.org.uk/CG111/NICEGuidance/pdf/English

Council for Disabled Children: *Including Me – Managing Complex Health Needs in Schools and Early Years Settings*
www.westsussex.gov.uk/idoc.ashx?docid=bd9e675d-7c1c-4369-8722-dbb2b3aca35a&version=-1

Department of Health: *Exemplar on Continence Issues for a Child with Learning Disabilities*
www.gov.uk/government/publications/national-service-framework-for-children-young-people-and-maternity-services-continence-issues-for-a-child-with-learning-difficulties

Practical resources
Radar Key
The UK National Key Scheme offers disabled people independent access to locked public toilets around the country. The National Key costs £4 from the Radar website; some local councils or carers centres may provide them without charge.

www.radar.org.uk or available from your local council offices.

Changing Places
Website with a list of toilets that are different to standard disabled toilets with extra features and more space to meet these needs.

www.changing-places.org

Just Can't Wait Toilet Card
Available from the Bladder and Bowel Foundation, this is a small, credit-sized card, designed to fit easily into your purse, wallet or pocket. You can show this card when you are out shopping and socialising and it may help you gain access to a toilet.

www.bladderandbowelfoundation.org
0845 345 0165

Toilet Time
Resource pack to help children understand toilet training.

www.sensetoys.com

Dry Like Me
Disposable toilet training pad that fits in a child's pants; helpful for toilet training and overflow soiling.

www.drylikeme.com

Squatty Potty
Toilet seat stool that goes around the base of a toilet to put the child in a squatting position.

www.squattypotty.co.uk

Portable Bidet
Sits under the toilet seat, useful for children who don't like the wee and poo dropping into the toilet.

www.fledglings.org.uk

Day wetting or bedwetting alarms

Body-worn alarms or sensor bed mats; may emit sound, vibration or a flashing glow when they detect wetness.

www.eric.org.uk

Vibrating watches

To use as memory triggers to go to the toilet.

www.eric.org.uk

Ideas and equipment to make toilet training fun or provide alternative sensory input!

Plop Trumps

Toilet Putty

Squeezy toys

Sensory fiddle toys

Stinky! Scratch & Sniff Stickers

Move 'n' Sit cushions

Therabands

Toilet Targets

Sand timers

Time Timer app

Books

For parents and practitioners

Cohn, A. (2007) *Constipation, Withholding and Your Child: A Family Guide to Soiling and Wetting.* London: Jessica Kingsley Publishers.

Coucouvanis, J.A. (2008) *The Potty Journey.* Shawnee Mission, KS: Autism Asperger Publishing Company.

Gray, C. (2010) *The New Social Story Book.* Arlington, TX: Future Horizons.

Laurie, C. (2013) *Sensory Strategies: Practical Ways to Help Children and Young People With Autism Learn and Achieve.* London: The National Autistic Society.

Singer, S. (n.d.) *Eat a Rainbow Every Day.* Available at www.eatarainboweveryday. com.

Wheeler, M. (1998) *Toilet Training for Individuals with Autism and Related Disorders.* Arlington, TX: Future Horizons.

Wrobel, M. (2003) *Taking Care Of Myself: A Healthy Hygiene, Puberty and Personal Curriculum For Young People With Autism.* Arlington, TX: Future Horizons.

Yack, E., Sutton, S., and Aquilla, P. (2002) *Building Bridges Through Sensory Integration: Therapy for Children with Autism and Other Pervasive Development Disorders.* Las Vegas, NV: Sensory Resources.

For children and young people

Bennett, H. (2007) *It Hurts When I Poop.* Washington, DC: Magination Press.

Black, T. (n.d.) *Poo Go Home.* Available at www.eric.org.uk.

Cho, S. (1994) *The Gas We Pass: The Story of Farts.* La Jolla, CA: Kane/Miller.

Daynes, K. (2006) *See Inside Your Body.* London: Usborne.

Goldsack, G. (2011) *The Pop Up Book of Poo.* London: Walker Books

Goldsmith, M. (2014) *In One End and Out the Other (Flip-Flap Journeys).* London: Red Shed.

Gomi, T. (2004) *Everyone Poos.* London: Frances Lincoln Children's Books.

Morgan, R. (2004) *Zoo Poo.* Hauppauge, NY: Barron's Educational Series.

Reynolds, K. (2014) *Ellie Needs to Go.* London: Jessica Kingsley Publishers.

Reynolds, K. (2014) *Tom Needs to Go.* London: Jessica Kingsley Publishers.

Smith, A. (1998) *Flip Flap Body Book.* London: Usborne.

Whelen-Banks, J. (2008) *Liam Goes Poo in the Toilet.* London: Jessica Kingsley Publishers.

Williams, I., and Wright, Y. (n.d.) *Sneaky Poo.* Available at www.eric.org.uk.

SUBJECT INDEX

Page numbers in *italics* refer to figures and charts.

AUTHOR INDEX